Teaching with Memories:
European Women's Histories in International
and Interdisciplinary Classrooms

First published May 2006
Women's Studies Centre
National University of Ireland, Galway
Galway
Ireland

ISBN: 0-9549924-4-X

Cover Design: A & D, Envision House, Flood Street, Galway
Cover Image: *Wasserbank* from Yugoslavia (private collection)

Typesetting and Design: Women's Studies Centre, National
University of Ireland, Galway
Printed by Cahill Printers, East Wall Road, Dublin 3

Teaching with Memories:
European Women's Histories in International
and Interdisciplinary Classrooms

Andrea Pető and Berteke Waaldijk, Editors

This publication has been made possible with the support of the Socrates/Erasmus Programme for Thematic Network Projects of the European Commission through grant number 110052-CP-1-2004-2-NL-ERASMUS for the ATHENA Advanced Thematic Network in Women's Studies in Europe.

Table of Contents

PART III – TEACHING EXPERIENCES

List of Illustrations

Foreword

In 1998 the European Union sponsored the creation of a Thematic Network on Teaching in Women's Studies. The Network was called 'ATHENA, Advanced Thematic Network in Activities in Women's Studies': the first stage ran from 1998 until 2002. ATHENA represented, for the first time in European history, a structured and permanent cooperation between scholars, experts and educators in the field of Women's Studies, Gender Studies and Feminist Studies. The objective was to assess and develop the interdisciplinary field of Gender, Feminist and Women's Studies in the framework of European integration. ATHENA aimed to research the current situation in the field of Women's Studies in Higher Education throughout Europe, identifying differences, strengths, weaknesses and areas of good practice. The panel devoted to teaching materials and best practices in teaching Women's Studies advised on elaborating forms of international co-teaching that would explicitly address differences among women. In the next stage of European Women's Studies cooperation, ATHENA 2 (2003-2006), several workgroups were devoted to experiments in co-teaching and the development of teaching modules. In the framework of the workgroup, 'Memories, Histories and Narratives' (ATHENA Workgroup 1b4, soon nicknamed one-be-four – 'the one before'), specialists interested in women's history met and worked for two years.[1] The objective of this workgroup was formulated as "the elaboration of the educational tool of foremother-research by students" as an element in international programmes. The working group discussed the assignment to search, find, share, and reflect on information about women from the students' social, intellectual, political and personal past.[2]

---

[1] This panel published "The Use of Women's Studies Teaching Books and Materials in Europe. A Comparative Report on Teaching Materials and Teaching Methods Used in Women's Studies Courses and Curricula in Different European Countries," in Braidotti *et al.*, (eds.), *The Making of European Women's Studies*, Vol. II, (Utrecht: Athena, Socrates Programme, European Commission, 2000).

[2] The following people have been members of the ATHENA Workgroup 1b4: Ann Lyons, Clara Moura Lorenco, Dietlind Huechtker, Francesca Brezzi, Giovanna Providenti, Gunilla Bjeren, Irina Novikova, Juliette Dor, Kristin Astgeirsdottir, Kristina Popova, Leena Kurvet, Maria Suarez Lafuente, Melita Richter, Nina Vodopivec, Renata Jambresic Kirin, Ritva Nätkin, Sonja Spee, Teresa Joaquim Adelina, Sanchez Espishosa, Rada Boric, Svetlana Slapsak, Patricia Chiantera-Stutte, Martine Jaminon, Lada Stevanovic, Jaana Vuori, Dalia Marcinkeviciene, Olga Stefanesca Doina, Mary Clancy.

The concept of foremothers has a long and impressive tradition in the teaching of Women's*Studies. Foremothers must be female family-members of an earlier generation; professional predecessors or inspiring examples and political heroines have been used. In this project, the experiences of this feminist pedagogic tradition are combined with the new possibilities of international and digitally-supported learning and teaching. The working group collected material, digital support and scholarly reflections on the possibilities of using the format of writing about 'foremothers' in different Women's and Gender Studies curricula. Writing and talking about them in the context of European and world history is an outstanding educational tool. It can be most effectively used and improved in situations where students from different national, cultural and ethnic backgrounds learn together.[3] Soon, the ATHENA workgroup, devoted to teaching the history of politically-active women in Europe[4] merged with Workgroup 1b4 on 'Memories, Histories, Narratives'. For two years, the members of the workgroup met and discussed their experiences of teaching with memories in classes, seminars, summer schools and non-academic projects. This book is one of the results.

Reflection about the lives of individual foremothers, who may be biologically or metaphorically related to the students, provides an excellent teaching tool. It provides diverse groups with the opportunity to discuss the core issues of writing women's history: the distinction between public and private lives, historiographical issues, as well as differences in experiences that may be defined nationally, religiously, ethnically, or in terms of class. Women's Studies programmes have a long tradition of teaching with reference to personal narratives. This was one of the reasons the 'Foremother Assignment' was introduced in several NOISE-summer schools.[5] When we claim that thinking about the histories of foremothers is a good starting point for discussing differences among women, it is clear that some of these differences may be benign and inspiring, while others touch the most painful parts of the European past: how

[3] See www.athena2.org for description.
[4] Workgroup 1b3: "Women and Extreme Political Parties, Movements in Europe: Anti-Europeanism, Identity and Populism".
[5] NOISE Summer Schools have been organised on a regular basis since 1996. In several of them, a cluster was devoted to women's history, and 'foremother-assignments,' in one way or another, were part of the programme.

should one address persecution, racism and violence while not forgetting about solidarity, love and friendship? The workgroup hoped to develop sophisticated means and forms to address these educational challenges.

The aim of the 'Memories, Histories and Narratives' workgroup was to provide material and digital support, scholarly reflection and examples of good practice on the use of the assignment of writing about 'foremothers' in different Women's Studies and Gender Studies curricula, as well as in projects that take place outside institutions of higher learning. Writing and talking about women with whom the students feel a special relationship is an outstanding educational tool. It allows students and teachers to address women's histories in the context of European and world history. It can be most effectively used and improved in situations where students from different national, cultural and ethnic backgrounds learn together: summer schools, where students and scholars from all over Europe meet, classes with students from different cultural, national and ethnic backgrounds, public history projects where people with different backgrounds meet. In the future, modules that use the foremother format will be part of international Women's Studies curricula.[6]

One of the aims of activity of ATHENA-Workgroup1b4 has been to train teachers in the use of this format. Thus, this project combines the experiences of this feminist pedagogic tradition with the new possibilities of international and digitally-supported learning and teaching. The participants in the workgroup collected and developed material that can be used in different contexts to teach about foremothers. The wide range of national backgrounds has provided the group with expertise about the ways the assignment may be conceived of in different national educational traditions.

This book is the result of two years of meetings and experiments in teaching. It combines work from scholars and teachers who explain how specific source material may be used in the classroom, and reports by scholars and teachers who have taught classes and used the foremother assignment. The book is not meant as the final word on teaching with memories. Rather, we hope it will be read as an invitation to explore the possibilities of international teaching of

---

[6] ATHENA2 and the proposed ATHENA3 will be working towards such curricula.

Women's and Gender Studies. We are aware that not all the possible sources have been mentioned, we are aware that many more fascinating teaching practices exist than what are described in this volume. We know that more books and articles on history, memory and narratives are available than what are mentioned in the bibliographies included here. However, we hope that the material collected here may find its way to teachers, scholars, students and everyone within and without the university who wants to teach the history of gender.

The articles in this collection have all been written on assignments relating to foremothers. Does this mean that the format is limited to the female sex? No. Gender is not limited to women: men's lives too are structured by gender. Assignments that ask students to explore the gender dimensions of male examples, such as great-grandparents and other predecessors, will undoubtedly also provide rich results. So would writing about 'fore-parents' along the lines of ethnicity, professional identity or class. The crucial element to us is that the life stories that are written by student-scholars will focus critically on the way dominant forms of history writing can be subverted. We have taken marginalised identities and used them to counter existing historical canons.

ATHENA European Thematic Network of Women's Studies provided us with the opportunity to try a classic format developed in feminist education, and we used it for teaching women's history in the context of European history. The redefintion of European history is a tool to break with the geographic definition of Europe and to find those elements and emotions that are constitutive forces of European identity. The meanings and contents of European identity are in constant flux, but they are also under serious challenges from populist and extreme right anti-European political forces. The ATHENA network, while connecting the European Women's Studies Centres, also serves as a niche for alternative teaching practices leading towards re-conceptualisation of European history, hence, offering a different meaning to European identity.

The assignment to write about a 'foremother' has a wealth of possibilities, among which we have only explored a few, but we feel confident in saying that for international training, in seminars where students and staff from different national educational systems come together, the format cannot be dispensed with. It also helps to address issues of differences from inside a national history by comparing experiences which, although coming from the same geographic unit, are entirely different. For example, comparing the life story of a Turkish or German woman in today's Germany or a Jewish or Hungarian woman in Hungary. Students become acquainted with the 'basics' of women's and feminist history. More important is the new form of empowerment it creates in students and teachers of Women's Studies. By making differences productive, and by making students author(itie)s before they enter the class room, this assignment gives students from different countries in Europe a chance to address their histories. The most interesting ways to further explore the prospects of the format include the impact of different media, used in presentations (paper, oral, digital, textual, visual), on the way students can experience the role of specialists and the interaction with other disciplines (one could imagine including questions in the assignment that come from the fields of sociology and cultural studies). In order to develop the format, it is necessary to list and evaluate systematically the material (the types of questions, supporting articles and books, the role of visits to women's centres) that has been inductive for the learning experiences for the students. This collection of articles is meant as a contribution to that process.

The accessibility of works in other countries would allow teachers to deal more effectively with the different educational backgrounds of students from different countries. Around this theme, discussion groups, even virtual discussion groups, could be set up between countries with conflicting interpretations of their past, aiming at reconciliation and conflict resolution (for instance, Hungary-Romania, Ireland-England, Serbia-Albania). Moreover, apart from this didactic aim, it would help to make the results of this form of student research available, thus collecting and opening these contributions to new women's histories about the European past in hope of a peaceful European future.

This book would not have been written and published without the support of many. At this point we would like to take the opportunity to thank all the students in the classes that are described in the texts. Moreover, we owe thanks to the ATHENA network, and the co-ordination office at the University of Utrecht, especially Rosi

Braidotti and Marlise Mensink. We would like to express our gratitude to the digital support team of the 2003 NOISE Summer School in Antwerp, namely Erna Kotkamp and Laurence Claeys. We are indebted to Utrecht University and Central European University, Budapest for material support, and to the EU Socrates Programme, for financial support. We are thankful for permission from publishers and archives to use texts and materials, and would also like to thank Izabella Agárdi and Rebecca Pelan for their extensive editing of the texts. Finally, this book would not have been published without the support of Ann Lyons, Mary Clancy, Rebecca Pelan, Vivienne Batt and the Women's Studies Centre, National University of Ireland, Galway.

On behalf of all contributors: Andrea Pető and Berteke Waaldijk.

PART I – INTRODUCTION

Memories, Histories and Narratives – Teaching With Memories in Europe.[7]

Berteke Waaldijk and Andrea Pető

The assignment to write about a foremother has a long history of producing and recognising knowledge about women in women's movements and different forms of feminism. The idea that women have a genealogy that differs from that of men, has a long tradition in feminism, and has dominated the field of women's history in its developing phases as an academic specialism. Jane Austen's complaint, voiced by one of the female characters in *Northanger Abbey*, that history was boring and uninspiring because it was all about "(t)he quarrels of popes and kings, with wars and pestilences, in every page; the men all so good for nothing, and hardly any woman at all,"[8] is only a prelude to two centuries of writers who argued that history, as it had been written by men, was incomplete.

The work of women's historians' *avant-la-lettre* at the turn of the nineteenth century (the American historian Mary Beard and the Dutch historian Johanna Naber, to mention just two names from a large group), describes histories of women who had been neglected by male historians, and addresses topics that did not make it into academic history written by men.[9] The attempts to remember her-stories,

---

[7] This article contains excerpts from our previous publications: Andrea Pető and Berteke Waaldijk, "Writing Women's Lives of Foremothers, The History and Future of a Feminist Teaching Tool," in Rosi Braidotti, Janny Niebert and Sanne Hirs (eds.), *The Making of the European Women's Studies*, Vol. 4. (ATHENA, Advanced Thematic Network in Activities in Women's Studies in Europe, Utrecht University, 2002), 149-162; Andrea Pető and Berteke Waaldijk, "Memories, Histories and Narratives" in Rosi Braidotti, Edyta Just and Marlise Mensink (eds.), *The Making of European Women's Studies*. Vol. 5. (U of Utrecht, 2004), 173-176; Berteke Waaldijk and Andrea Pető, "A női példaképek élettörténetének írása. A feminista pedagógiai eszköz története, gyakorlata és jövője," (Writing Stories of Foremothers. History, Practice and Future of a Feminist Pedagogical Tool) in *Új Pedagógiai Szemle* (2005, 2.), 3-16. http://www.oki.hu/cikk.php?kod=2005-02-ta-Tobbek-Noi.html

[8] Jane Austen, *Northanger Abbey*, (Hammondsworth, Penguin Books, 1985), (first published in 1815), 123.

[9] On Mary Beard: Bonnie Smith, "Seeing Mary Beard," in *Feminist Studies* 10.3 (Fall 1984): 399-416; on Johanna Naber: Maria Grever, *Strijd tegen de Stilte. Johanna Naber (1859-1941) en de vrouwenstem in de geschiedenis*, (Struggle Against the Silence. Johanna Naber (1859-1941) and the Women's Voice in History) (Verloren: Hilversum, 1994); Maria Grever, "The Pantheon of Feminist Culture: Women's Movements and the Organization of Memory," in *Gender and History* Vol. 9. No. 2: 364-374.

however, were not limited to the genre of academic writing. Women have used a great variety of genres to keep alive memories of a female past: from telling and re-telling stories, singing songs, and making quilts, to writing novels, family memoirs and academic dissertations.[10] With the resurgence of the women's movement in the last quarter of the twentieth century, these traditions re-surfaced and helped the beginning of Women's Studies as an academic field. Remembering and re-telling the history of one's mother and grandmother was one of the elements in the feminist consciousness-raising groups that flowered in the US and Western Europe,[11] and the idea that the history of women could be told and documented through private memories and stories contributed to a re-thinking of the distinction and the hierarchy between private and public.

In the former Soviet Block during the period of communism, the past was distorted to legitimise communist rule, and history was narrowed down to an enforced forgetting. Women, therefore, remembering their lives in print, followed the canonised hagiographic version of Party history.[12] In the past twelve years in Eastern Europe, we have witnessed a boom in the publishing of memories in books and journals, but very few of them are written by women.[13] After the fall of communism in Eastern Europe, 'private' knowledge and 'private' histories were used to challenge official representations and to recover 'the real history' without the State/Party-orchestrated distortion. In Eastern European countries, different oral history collections were set up, collecting 'private' sources opposing the

---

[10] Hazel Carby, *Reconstructing Womanhood,* (New York: Oxford UP., 1987); Lawrence Levine, *Black Culture and Black Consciousness* (1977); Gianna Pomata, *"Partikulargeschichte und Universalgeschichte - Bemerkungen zu eingen Handbüchern der Frauengeschichte,"* in *L'homme Z.F.G.* 2 (1990), 5-44. [also published as: Gianna Pomata, "History, Particular and Universal: Some Recent Women's History Textbooks" *Feminist Studies* 19. 1 (Spring 1993), 7-50].; Natalie Zemon.Davis, "Gender and Genre: Women as Historical Writers, 1400-1820," in P.H. Labalme (ed.), *Beyond Their Sex. Learned Women of the European Past,* (New York UP., 1980), 153-182.

[11] Robin Morgan, *Sisterhood is Powerful: An Anthology of Writings from the Women's Liberation Movement,* (New York: Random House, 1973).

[12] Andrea Pető, "Women's Life Stories. Feminist Genealogies in Hungary," in Slobodan Naumovic and Miroslav Jovanovic, (eds.), *Gender Relations in South Eastern Europe. Historical Perspectives on Womanhood and Manhood in 19th and 20th Century,* (Zur Kunde Suedosteuopas-Band II/33: Belgrad-Graz, 2002), 211-219.

[13] Andrea Pető, "Writing Women's History in Eastern Europe. Toward a "Terra Cognita?" *Journal of Women's History* 16 (4) 2004, 173-183.

'public'/official sources, assuming that 'public' sources were all 'wrong.' It is crucial to understand the 'metaphoric mapping' of these private memories in order to break out from the 'true/false' framework of remembering, which prevails today. The post-1989 period was also expected to re-define gender relations in the democratisation process. During communism, the stereotypical women's characteristics were intimacy, sensitivity, and family-centredness, perceived as resistance to 'statist feminism'.[14] The private resistance to communism rested on the restoration of the so-called 'female virtues' in families, based on the three expected roles of women as daughters, wives and mothers. This attempt, which had religious ideological support, aimed to preserve the family values in private life against the pseudo-gender equality of state socialism.[15] After 1989, a restoration of 'female virtues' could be observed, which neither modified institutions in the ways gender hierarchies are performed and institutionalised, nor in the ways in which women are placed or, rather, mis-placed from national narratives.

The argument of early women's historians was that the history of women was invisible[16] because official history only described the public sphere while women's history took place in the private sphere, where women had been delegated. Women's stories were not visible; women's stories were not told, such were the sad observations of those historians who aimed to recover women's political agency in history. Many post-1989 history books about Eastern European history, and written by men, do not include those topics that are important for national history writing, such as mother/daughter relationships, women's friendships, women working together, women in love with women.[17] Feminist histories of child-care, sexuality,

---

[14] Andrea Pető, "'As He Saw Her': Gender Politics in Secret Party Reports in Hungary During 1950s," in *CEU History Department Working Paper Series* No.1. (1994), 107-121.

[15] See Andrea Pető, "Conservative and Extreme Right Wing Women in Contemporary Hungary. An Ideology in Transition," in Knezevic, Durdja, Koraljka Dilic (eds.), *Women and Politics. Women in History/History Without Women,* (Zagreb: Zenska Infoteka, 2001), 265-277.

[16] Renate Bridenthal, Claudia Koonz, Susan Stuard, (eds.), *Becoming Visible: Women in European History,* (Boston: Houghton Mifflin, 1977 and 1987).

[17] For an exception, see: Kristina Popova, Petar Vodenicharov, Snezhana Dimitrova, (eds.), *Women and Men in the Past. 19th and 20th Century. Additional Teaching Material for Secondary Schools,* International Seminar for Balkan Studies and Specialisation, (Blagoevgrad: South Western University, 2002) translated into the 9 languages of South Eastern Europe and used in secondary level of teaching history.

household technologies, and the cult of domesticity, documented a history that, for some, had been the core of the lives of their mothers and grandmothers. Different forms of an assignment that asked students to look into the history of their mothers, grandmothers and (grand-)aunts were integrated in early courses of Women's Studies and women's history.

We feel ourselves indebted to and inspired by this tradition and have worked with the format in different contexts ourselves. In 1987, Berteke Waaldijk integrated the assignment to write a paper about the life of a female ancestor in a course called 'Between Margin and Centre, Women and Cultural Traditions'. Andrea Pető taught a version of the assignment at the Department of Gender Studies at Central European University, Budapest in the Winter Term of 2004, and in several seminars with the explicit aim of introducing students to the methodology of oral history.[18] The foremother stories used in these classes and seminars represent an emotional opportunity to tell a story that might help the participants to think about themselves in different historical terms, and also help them to understand how the national, canonised history taught in the history textbooks is connected to personal histories. The essays the participants wrote helped them to recover the intellectual and emotional 'matrilineage' and to reconstruct broken feminist genealogies. Our experiences with the assignment, used in these last two summer schools, are described in detail in Part III of this book.

Here, we want to elaborate, in general, what students and educators can learn from teaching with memories. We have based this

---

[18] In September 1998 the inaugurating conference of the Association of Teaching Gender Studies in Eastern Europe was organised by the Open Society Institute Women's Network Programme in Belgrade, which was followed by the conference 'Women's History and History of Gender in Countries in Transition' in Minsk. The conference papers were published in Elena Gapova, Al'mira Usmanova, Andrea Pető, (eds.), *Gendernye istorii Vostochnoy Evropi* (Gendered Histories from Eastern Europe), (European Minsk: Humanities University, 2002). These two conferences gave a picture of the present state of feminist scholarship in history in Eastern Europe, and it also signalled possible directions and policies for the future, so the Open Society Institute Network Women Programme started a series of feminist oral history training workshops: in Budapest (2000), in Azerbaijan, Moldova and Kirgiztan (2001), in Armenia and in a summer school in Kirgiztan (2002). During these workshops, Andrea Pető used the foremother assignment. Andrea Pető, (ed.), *To Look at Life through Women's Eyes: Women's Oral Histories from the Former Soviet Union*, (New York: Network Women's Program, Open Society Institute, 2002), 33.

reflection on the possibilities of the foremother assignment on discussions with colleagues, with students, and on courses that we have taught ourselves. We will distinguish between aspects of gender history, aspects of feminist theory, and aspects of the more pedagogical – some would say political – nature of empowering students.

Women's History

Reflection about the lives of individual foremothers (whether they are biologically or otherwise related to the students) provides an excellent opportunity to discuss two core issues of writing women's history: the distinction between public and private lives, and historiography. Let us begin with the distinction between public and private. As one of the oldest concepts used in women's history, we believe feminist scholars should be aware of the advantages and limits of using this opposition. The advantages are well known: facts of women's lives that have received no public recognition were assigned to the personal sphere, which, in itself, was supposed to have no history. Students recognise this clearly when they are asked to think about what elements of the foremother's lives could be found in official history books since, mostly, these hardly exist.

However, women's historians have formulated important critiques of the value of the gender distinction between the male public and the female public sphere. As it was pointed out, "liberating women from the domestic sphere" was a political and historiographic ideal that was mainly directed at middle class women in Western Europe and the US.[19] For many women, the 'cult of domesticity' was not the issue. African-American women who lived in slavery struggled together with African-American men for the right to have a private sphere and a family life. Women in communist societies did not experience the private sphere as the site of their oppression. Working class women often combined wage-earning with the care of a family. The assignment to study the life of a foremother allows students to think about the distinction between public and private, as well as consider the advantages and drawbacks of the concept.

---

[19] Berteke Waaldijk, "Of Stories and Sources: Feminist History," in Rosemarie Buikema and Anneke Smelik (eds.), *Women's Studies and Culture,* (London: Zed Books, 1994), 14-25.

The second important issue that assignments about foremothers allow is the history of feminism, women's movements and other struggles for emancipation. Whether or not questions about feminism are explicitly included in the assignment, one can see that in almost every classroom discussion about the history of women, the history of women's emancipation naturally arises. Students reflect on differences in the social, civil and political rights of women, and they ask where changes in this field come from.

In the third place, the assignment to study the life story of a foremother enables critical reflection about the way history is being written. This historiographical focus, always strong in the field of women's history, and one that combines empirical research with feminist theory, is often a difficult topic to teach, especially to students who have not been trained as historians. It is too easy to present a simplified opposition between bad history books, in general, that do not pay attention to women in history, and the feminist alternatives. However, it seems clear that students will learn much more about this problem when they are invited to think about the distinction between national historiography and their own specific interest in an individual woman.

Questions aimed at reflecting upon the ways in which the foremothers were integrated or excluded from national histories are, therefore, crucial in teaching with memories, as are the questions about the resources available for more knowledge about a foremother's life. The reinvention of the wheel should not be the aim of any assignment. These questions allow teachers to make use of work done by women's historians. These questions make students aware of the various roles in which women can be integrated in general histories: as victims, as heroes, as survivors, as marginalised outsiders, or as metaphors of national identities. The work of Gianna Pomata on particular and general history has been very useful in this context, as it helps to make students aware of the different perspectives that structure the way they write about women.[20]

No teaching of women's history can do without making the students acquainted with the sources and resources that are available. While trained historians can envisage the limits and possibilities of the

---

[20] Pomata, *ibid*.

source material that they have been trained to use, starters in the field will have very little knowledge. By asking students, from the very beginning, to report about the different sources they have used to write the story about their foremother, the issue of availability of sources is made urgent. Students will experience what it means to write about events that have not made it into history books; they may feel proud about unearthing material that nobody has used before (talking to relatives, looking at pictures), and they will begin to experience the enormous need for work in the field, of collecting material for the untold histories about women in the past. A visit to a women's archive, or a women's information centre is, therefore, a crucial element in the assignment.[21] It will confront the students with the politics of remembering, conservation, and the way material objects are opened up for historical research. One of the most striking elements when reading about teaching with memories is the wealth of different objects that enter the classroom: historical research is no longer only about books and archives, but also about dresses, photographs, furniture, jewellery, food and recipes.

Finally, students who have to write and present the life story of a foremother will become aware of the responsibility that everyone who writes history has: the power to include and to exclude. Students, in a class where all students carry out the assignment, have to discuss, present and compare the histories of women with the stories about women in other countries, in other classes, and of other ethnicities. The fact that histories are written from different perspectives is very tangible. Students are, thus, invited, if not forced, to reflect on the way their story affects others.

Feminist Theory and Interdisciplinarity

Teaching with memories is not limited to teaching classes in women's history. It is also a useful tool for explaining elements in feminist theory. The problematisation of 'experience' is especially crucial when a group of Women's Studies students with different national and academic background work together. For beginners in the field of women's history, it is sometimes tempting to expect that women's

---

[21] This may be real-life or virtual through one of the electronically available centres. The oral history projects of the OSI NWP are located in the different Women's Studies Centres and documentation centres in Eastern Europe and Central Asia.

experiences have been basically the same in different eras and in different locations. The critical work done by Women's Studies specialists who addressed not only discrimination and subjection on the basis of sex, but investigated the ways in which race, class and sexuality have interacted with gender, has made abundantly clear that there is no such thing as 'the woman's experience'. Several authors have made the theoretical elaboration of this point. We mention here the article "Experience" by Joan Scott, who criticises the way 'experience' has been seen as the indubitable fundament of emancipation movements. She shows why feminism should move away from this absolute belief in an independent subject who is influenced by experiences, and argues for a view that pays more attention to the ways in which some events are being turned into 'experiences', while others remain untold. For students in Women's Studies, this lesson is valuable because it allows them to reflect on the responsibility of constructing a story.[22] Other theoretical issues may be addressed via life stories: theories of sex and gender, theoretical work on the body, on intersectionality, on performativity, or on subjectivity can be included.

The assignment to study and write the life stories of foremothers offers good opportunities for interdisciplinary cooperation as a highly important feature of Women's Studies. It allows students who are trained in different disciplines (sociology, cultural or literary studies, history, economics, political sciences, media studies) to use this knowledge in working on the assignment. Because the questions asked about the foremother can and should cover a wide range of facts, students are invited to use the knowledge. This happens most productively when in-class comparisons are being made: students can discuss the differences between industrial and agricultural countries and regions, they evaluate class differences and cultural developments that have not stopped at national borders. In an international class, students can discuss films and novels that have been shared by women in different countries, they can compare the way fashion is an issue between different generations of women and, in doing this, they

---

[22] Joan Scott, "Experience," in Joan Scott, Judith Butler, (eds.), *Feminists Theorize the Political* (New York: Routledge, 1992), 22-40; See, also, Denise Riley, *Am I that Name. Feminism and the Category of 'Women in History'*, (London: MacMillan, 1988).

discover that private lives were deeply embedded in inter- or trans-national structural developments.

Feminist Pedagogies – Empowering the Student-Author

One of the greatest challenges of teaching Women's, Gender or Feminist Studies in an international and multicultural context, is to make the diversity within the classroom productive, instead of an impediment, to teaching. Many international seminars have experienced serious problems of non-cooperation across national, cultural and ethnic lines and have had difficulty in setting up meaningful frames for trans-national comparisons. Education is so thoroughly intertwined with the way students and teachers see the world. Different language-proficiency, differences in expectations about the role of the teacher, or the role of the students in the classroom, can literally destroy learning experiences. Political differences will add tensions and conflicts in the class. In one of the early NOISE-Summer Schools, a session was devoted to introducing national differences through songs and national anthems. Some teachers had expected that women from all European countries would be critical towards all forms of nationalism, including that of their own country, but they were proved very wrong. Indeed, as we can see now, it would be an illusion to expect women to be unaffected by histories of genocide, discrimination and subjection, directed at their nation, race or ethnic group.[23] The challenge for international teaching programmes in Women's Studies is to create environments where the differences among students and among teachers can be made productive.

The assignment to present the life of foremothers will help educators meet this challenge. Unmediated, students must write about an aspect of their history without having to address their own position. The displacement allows students and teachers to speak about racism and imperialism as crucial issues in European history without being paralysed by national definitions of guilt. The assignment can also be used in gender sensitivity training in classrooms where serious resistance is expected against anything related to feminism and to women's movements. This resistance,

---

[23] Rosi Braidotti and Gabriele Griffin, (eds.), *Thinking Differently. A Reader in European Women's Studies*, (London: Zed Books, 2002).

mainly due to the epistemic character of the Cold War (in some Eastern European classrooms) and/or the feeling that liberal capitalism has emancipated Western women (in some Western European classrooms), can be successfully challenged through the introduction of personalised histories connected to women's experiences.[24]

Related to this form of empowering students to address the big issues in European and world history, is the form of empowerment for students that results from having them enter the classroom as 'authors'. This assignment addresses students as specialists, since they are the only ones who know about their 'foremother'. This means that students can enter the discussion, not only as learners, but also as 'teachers'. This point is particularly important in bringing together different national traditions of education: while some countries have a tradition of training students not to accept what their teachers tell them, other countries don't. In some countries teachers are trained to see discussions and seminars where students contribute their knowledge and views as the core of the curriculum, in others the lecture format is more central. These differences are related to different styles of authority in different countries. Within feminist pedagogies there exists a strong tradition of the ideal of empowering students.[25] The production of foremother's stories has a spiritual dimension: it is a reconstruction of identity because it helps us to believe that no outside or interiorised approval is needed to please others, and it also purges those stories that are imposed on women by the dominant traditions.

By creating open stories, the format of writing the life stories of women can help to construct or repair the missing or distorted continuity between generations of women. When we go by our own experience with international summer schools, where both staff and students come from different educational systems, it is crucial to explicitly address different ways of dealing with authority. If this is not done, patterns may be repeated. Making students into specialists and turning them into student-scholars is a good beginning.

---

[24] Andrea Pető, "Writing Women's History," in *Open Society News*, (Fall 1994), 10-11.
[25] Ellen Carol Dubois, *et. al.* (eds.), *Feminist Scholarship. Kindling in the Groves of Academia*, (Urbana UP., 1985); bell hooks, *Teaching to Transgress. Education as the Practice of Freedom*, (New York: Routledge, 1994).

Finally, we think it is important to point out that empowering students in the classroom will also help them to create their own voices *vis-à-vis* the 'big narratives' of European history. A history that is permeated by so much violence, dictatorship, and exploitation, needs students who feel they can tell other stories and formulate alternatives. They may, thus, contribute to the alternatives of protest and idealism that have also been part of European history. Analysing women's life stories is an attempt to give a voice to women's stories that cannot be dismissed as false generalisation within the 'big narratives'. This methodological approach is more about understanding and opening than about controlling and closure. Changing the narrative framework and the social dimension of remembering gives a new orientation in the world and attracts respect for equality and freedom.

PART II – SOURCES

Introduction

Students who start writing a life story about a foremother will have to find out how and where this life is remembered. One of the crucial elements in this phase of the assignment and the teaching process is to make clear that histories, memories and narratives about lives in the past can be found at various locations. Teachers may suggest where to look for memories. This is a moment where students become aware of differences between 'public memories' and 'private memories'. They will learn to distinguish between descriptions of events that have been written down in official reports, in newspapers, in history books, and those that are kept in diaries and private letters. This is a moment when the teachers may assign readings in women's history that deal with the public-private distinction. In many cases, students will be able to have a conversation with the foremother they describe, or with people who have known her. They will then be interested in what it means to do oral history, they will have to think of effective ways to start conversations about the past, and they will reflect on the 'situatedness' of memories. Many books and articles are available to support this exploration of constructing narratives about the past. Depending on the context, the instructor may make these available to the students, before, during or after their endeavors.

In our experience, it is important to suggest possibilities for finding memories. For the experienced women's historian, it is clear that many different sources provide access to the past, but for many students this is still a surprise. They may have been trained to see history as the result of research in official archives that can be found in history books.

To help students and teachers to imagine the wealth of sources that are available for the authors of historical life stories, we have collected a series of fourteen examples of source material. They have been described by scholars who have actually used these sources in the context of reconstructing life stories. The short essays in this part of the book contain the description of a specific source, and of the genre to which it belongs, as well as an elaboration of the information that may be gathered from such a source. These examples are by no means exhaustive: they are merely meant to indicate some different possibilities. The sources have been arranged in four categories: 'public sources,' 'objects,' 'texts,' and 'conversations.' We start with a description of 'public' memories: official texts from governments, the police, the military and a labor contract. It is insightful to see how much information about 'ordinary' people can be gathered from official texts. Using them will train students in taking into account the goal with which those texts were written, the hidden meanings and power relations that have an impact on their meaning.

The official texts are followed by what we call objects: material things that carry history. This may be a monument, a photograph, a birthday card, or a piece of furniture. These sources share their materiality: students may see, touch, and handle them. Material objects – and one can also think of a piece of jewellery, a dress, a kitchen utensil, a pen – are often very helpful in interviews: they trigger memories long forgotten, and they may have been seen, touched and handled by different people. This will allow students to compare different ways of remembering. Regarding visual sources, such as photographs, film and pictures, the teacher may also utilise expertise in visual studies.

Texts come to us in the form of books, letters, transcripts, publications, and these are as material as pictures and statues. We continue the list of sources with these specific material objects. We have collected sources that consist of texts as a separate category. The examples of private letters, autobiographies, a published diary and novels require from students who use them as a source for the life story of their foremother, the additional expertise of how to read and analyse textual sources. Students with a background in literary studies will possess such expertise.

The last category of sources that we present is identified as conversations. The chosen examples refer to interviews, one of them published and available to the students, the other an example of an interview conducted by the researcher herself. In many contexts, interviews are already available, either in popular magazines or published in books, in oral histories, or in ethnographic collections. Students may use these interviews or they may conduct them themselves. The great educational advantage of such a source is that it makes students aware of the position of the interviewer, and her role in the construction of knowledge about the past.

We hope that this series of fourteen examples will inspire students and teachers to use the wide variety of source material that can be used to write foremother histories.

Public Sources

1. *Minutes of an Official Meeting*
   Andrea Pető

Illustration: Photo of Júlia Rajk and László Rajk
(private collection, with permission of the owner)

The Source

> Kádár János: The press release about the funeral was nonsense. Was this made by us?
>
> Óvári Miklós: Us?
>
> KJ.: Well, we announced that she died, and we buried her.
>
> OM.: That was brief, indeed.
>
> KJ.: This is a total nonsense, that was just the same what was announced on the day when she died. Why did not they put down, that on Monday she was buried here or there. A speech was given by this or that. Have not they dared to put it down? Excuse me… By the way did it go O.K.?
>
> OM.: It was O.K. Approx. 500 people were there.[26]

---

[26] Magyar Országos Levéltár (Hungarian National Archive, MOL, 288.f. 5/836.), 71-72.

Background

This quotation is from the Minutes of the Hungarian Socialist Worker's Party *Politburo* meeting on 15 September, 1981.[27] The discussion refers to the death of an important person. In the original text, in Hungarian, the sex of the buried person is not clear, but in the English translation it is obvious that the most powerful leaders of communist Hungary were discussing the death and the funeral of a woman. The person who was asking questions during the meeting was János Kádár, who determined the history of Hungary between 1956 and 1989 (called 'The Kádár years'). In 1949, János Kádár was a Minister of Interior and he was responsible for murdering the husband of the deceased woman. Her name was not mentioned during the whole meeting, but everybody knew who she was.

There was only one woman in Hungarian history whose destiny was to know, as personal enemies, the two most influential Hungarian politicians of the post Second World War period, Mátyás Rákosi and János Kádár. Together, they masterminded the execution of her husband after a show trial in 1949. The husband, László Rajk, was a legendary fighter in the Spanish Civil War, leader of the home-grown communist movement in Hungary, and iron-fisted Minister of Interior of Hungary.

In Hungary in the post Second World War period (1949-1989), there were two names that were silenced. After the execution of the holders of these names, they were erased from documents and history, air-brushed from photographs, and those who knew them in person feared imprisonment and execution for pronouncing these names loudly. The first name was László Rajk, whose rehabilitation and reburial on 6 October, 1956 proved to be a rehearsal for the Hungarian Revolution of 23 October, 1956. The second name was Imre Nagy, the Prime Minister of the Hungarian Revolution, who was also executed by order from János Kádár in 1958. Milan Kundera characterised the resistance against communism as a fight with power of memory against forgetting. In twentieth century Hungarian history, no-one else fought with such eloquence against the official versions of forgetting as did Júlia Rajk. She had to fight to restore her own name, the name of her son, and the name of her husband against forgetting.

---

[27] These Minutes are held in Magyar Országos Levéltár, Budapest (Hungarian National Archive 288.f. 5/836, 71-72).

The Heroine

Júlia Rajk was born as Júlia Földes in 1914 in a lower working class family with a strong communist tradition. Between 1945 and 1949, as wife of the famous communist Minister of Interior, Lászlóné Rajk (Mrs. László Rajk), she was one of the leaders of the mass communist women's organisation. In 1949, after the execution of her husband, she was sentenced to five years imprisonment for supporting her husband's so called 'subversive policy'. After her sentence, she was released from prison as Lászlóné Györk (Mrs. László Györk). Her and her son's names were changed without any consultation in an attempt to obliterate the name of her husband. Her appeals for official rehabilitation to the leaders of the Communist Party were signed by both names Rajk and Györk. She used her unquestionable and uncontested moral power as a widow of the innocently executed hero of the Hungarian communist movement, to force the Communist Party leadership into starting and completing the rehabilitation of political prisoners, and her husband was buried with all possible official honours on 6 October, 1956. The photo of the widow and her son, taken at the funeral, became world famous as a symbol of victims of Stalinism. The son was a three-month-old baby when his father was imprisoned. The baby was taken to an orphanage and his name was changed to István Kovács, a common Hungarian name. After the reburial, the widow and her son regained their names of Lászlóné Rajk and László Rajk jr., respectively.

On 4 November, 1956, when the Soviet army occupied Hungary, Júlia Rajk asked for political refugee status at the Embassy of Yugoslavia, together with Imre Nagy, the Prime Minister of the Hungarian Revolution of 1956, and the members of his cabinet. Júlia was kidnapped by the Soviets and taken to Romania, together with Imre Nagy, where she spent two years until she was given permission to return to Hungary as Júlia Rajk. After 1958, she became 'the' Júlia, a real institution, who always protected the weak against those who were abusing their power. She negotiated with the Party leadership to protect the anti-communist intellectuals, and she organised the first NGO in Hungary after the ban on associations in 1951. She founded a dog shelter, and also organised signatures for supporting the Charta 77, and campaigned against strengthening the abortion law. She donated the compensation she received for the loss of her husband to a fund supporting talented university students at a time when individual charity was not an accepted value.

Júlia Rajk would have disliked being named as a feminist because, for her, it would have meant a liberal middle class woman following the judgement of the communist movement. When the first proto-feminist movement was organised against the strengthening of abortion laws in 1975, Ms Rajk was the first to sign the petition, giving explicit support, through her name, to the first dissent action organised in Hungary after 1956. I would name her the most successful Hungarian feminist so far, if we take into consideration the influence and impact of her actions, which were protected with her name, and executed in her presence.

To Be Learned
Name, naming, construction of political subjectivity, women's activism during communism

Assignment
> ➤ List women who you know 'made their name' in a totalitarian context of fighting for rights.
> ➤ Identify the techniques of domination from the source.
> ➤ Read the text Denise Riley, *'Am I that Name?' Feminism and the Category of 'Women' in History*,[28] and discuss the construction of female subjectivity in history.
> ➤ Identify the main historical characters in the life story and try to find information on them in your own country. What conclusions can you draw on memory and forgetting?
> ➤ Analyse the leftist tradition in your country, where can you place women's issues there in the inter-war period, after the Second World War, in the 1980s and today? What makes the difference, if any?

---

[28] Denise Riley, *'Am I that Name?' Feminism and the Category of 'Women' in History*, (Macmillan, 1988).

2.   Census Manuscript: Public Record – Personal Source
Mary Clancy

Illustration: The Chestnut household
(Census of Ireland, 1901, County Galway, 47/38)

Context and Description

The census manuscript is a versatile source of information. Its function, to gather the vital statistics of a country's population in a systematic fashion, means that there is a public record for each citizen. In turn, researchers have a right to view such manuscripts in public archives. In Ireland, for instance, researchers have access to the 1901 and the 1911 census manuscripts held in the National Archives in Dublin. In addition, local county libraries and universities hold selected microfilm copies and, increasingly, census data is available on-line. Additionally, those searching for information about emigrant life histories must consult the records of host countries. English records, for instance, are important sources in an Irish context. Electronic databases are an excellent aid, though sight of the original document is suggested, if possible. The chief constraint is availability, especially where records and public buildings are destroyed during war. This happened in Ireland, for instance, in 1922 and, so, with rare exceptions, there are no extant Irish census records for the nineteenth century.

Scope and Value

The census document contains categories of information, including name and surname, relation to head of family, religious profession, education, age, sex, rank, profession or occupation, marriage, where born, and whether suffering physical or other medical conditions. The census of Ireland also contained a column about ability to speak the Irish language. The 1911 census had an additional column seeking information about years of marriage, the number of children born, and the number of children still living. These categories, then, suggest something of the potential of the census as a source of information in constructing life histories.

The most obvious value of this source is its function in reconstructing individual biography. As noted already, census categorisation offers a valuable starting point into finding out when women married or gave birth. Some of the information, however, is problematic. Historians of women's work, like Caitriona Clear,[29] have written about the rigidity and ill-defined nature of official concepts like 'gainfully employed' and 'engaged in home duties'. It is also possible, however, to analyse the available information in order to determine the range of tasks and responsibilities within the household and to use the scope of the census to situate women's role or space within a household. Researchers can examine questions about social class relationships in middle or upper-class households, caring for elderly or ill family members, informal fostering of children, and the migration of women into new households on marriage. The census is exceptionally important as a document about domestic servants, a category of worker that is surprisingly ignored,[30] despite the prevalence of this occupation for working class girls and women.

The census is also especially useful as a tool for gathering information about groups who do not ordinarily leave written records. Its democratic value allows the researcher to write life histories of the poor and the working classes – social classes that are often represented only as statistics without names. Some, like those in prison, asylums or reformatories, are counted only as initials; an anonymity that is a

---

[29] Caitriona Clear, *Women of the House: Women's Household Work in Ireland, 1926-1961*, (Dublin: Irish Academic Press, 2000), see, in particular, Chapter 1, 13-26.

[30] One important study is Mona Hearn, *Below Stairs: Domestic Service Remembered in Dublin and Beyond, 1880-1922*, (Dublin: The Lilliput Press, 1993).

powerful statement about identity and visibility, respectability and status within the society in question.

Accuracy

The completed census document has value beyond the recording of data. For instance, the recording of false information, whether intentionally or not, offers important insight into human behaviour. Information about age and literacy is often inaccurate, as cross-checking with other documents (including subsequent census reports) reveals. People may not have known their exact age, for instance. Where those who were not literate required others to fill in the form, then accuracy must be questioned. As analysis of manuscripts reveals, typically in such instances, local teachers, shopkeepers, literate neighbours or school children helped to write up the family's details. The inability of the enumerator to speak the language of the household in Irish speaking areas, or the inability of an employer to report the biographical details of domestic servants in large households, similarly, suggests the importance of taking a critical approach to interpreting the details. Essentially, however, the census was an instrument of state enquiry and, while others helped, the local policeman was the official enumerator. The official nature of the source must be borne in mind, then, when analysing the type of information that is proffered. For the student of women's suffrage, the 1911 census also offers the complex challenge of tracking those feminists who evaded the census in the 1911 suffrage campaign against census enumeration. Feminists also recorded on the census form their objection to being without the parliamentary vote.

Assignment

The census, as noted, is a basic instrument in foremother research. It can stimulate questions about roles and identity or it can confirm information derived from oral and family sources. The census-based assignment is also an excellent method of encouraging students to think about the complexities of how personal information is shaped and transmitted, hidden and subverted, on a public record.

Use a copy of family or other census manuscript to explore the following questions:

> ➢ Write a report on how the personal and the public are located on the same document.
> ➢ Discuss how acquiring a family census manuscript has changed existing knowledge about foremother or family.
> ➢ Discuss the value of the census as a source of information about gender and literacy.
> ➢ Discuss the ethical issues involved in census based research.
> ➢ What does the census reveal about women's professional, casual and household work? In this the student should offer a critique of formal census classification and try to infer, on the basis of other evidence in the document, the type of domestic, caring and other work undertaken by women.

Illustration

The example used to illustrate a census manuscript is that of the Chestnut household. It is of initial interest as an all-female, relatively young household, its nine inhabitants claiming three different religions. The place of birth of household members extends to India, an apt reminder of the occupational and political mobility of these subjects of the British empire.

The general domestic servant to the household, M. G. is the only local girl and the only catholic, situating her in an interesting minority space within a county where most are born locally and approximately 97% is catholic[31]. The nurse to the household, who also operates as domestic servant, is protestant, suggesting something of the sectarian sensitivities of the household in relation to working with children, an area much contested, on religious grounds, in the Ireland of this era. The nurse, who is from the same county as the Chestnut sisters, points, too, to the mobility required of working class women and the practice of finding household staff through local or home contacts. Questions may be asked of her qualifications at a time when nursing was emerging as an occupation requiring formal training and certification, a shift marked in twentieth century census classification

---

[31] Information is derived from Census of Ireland, 1901 and 1911.

that now placed nursing in the professional category of the census rather than in the domestic, as formerly. Strangely, in a household concerned with education, there is no reference to speaking Irish. It is likely, for instance, that M.G., the local general servant, had knowledge of Irish, yet Agnes Chestnut decided either not to ask her or to ignore the question.

Such documents also invite researchers to probe the possible dynamics of such households. How did the relatively young Chestnut sisters treat their staff, for instance? How did the two twenty-year-old domestic servants work together? Did religious difference affect their status within the household or with each other? How did the seventeen-year-old boarder, Violet, get along with staff? How did the arrival of the Henderson family from India, with three small children, affect the equilibrium and work of the household? Clearly, to fully appreciate the social, intellectual, religious and political weighting and world of this household, other sources are required. In this case, for instance, the census document will not yield the important fact that the Chestnut sisters had established a ladies' day school in Galway in October, 1888.[32] The school aimed to educate girls to university level, an academic path that only became available in Ireland in the late 1870s.[33] Over the coming decades, the High School educated local protestant girls (catholic middle class girls attended the Dominican convent school), preparing the first generation of women to enter the local university.

---

[32] *Galway Express*, 20th Oct. 1888.

[33] See, for instance, Mary Cullen, *Girls Don't Do Honours: Irish Women in Education in the 19th and 20th Centuries* (Dublin: Women's Education Bureau, 1987).

3.   Military Report
María Suárez Lafuente

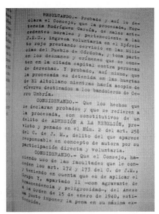

Illustration: Military Report in Dulce Chacón, La voz dormida.
(Madrid, Alfaguara, 2002), 221-222.

The Source

> […]It has been PROVED, as the Council declares, that the prisoner, Hortensia Rodríguez García, with a dubious moral past and a member of the J.S.U. (Socialist Youth United), had joined the Red Army voluntarily, was active in the Folk Militia of Córdoba, took part in the riots and crimes committed against people affected to the Nationalists in the aforementioned capital city. And proved, likewise, that the accused has been taken up in the El Altollano gardens while she was procuring food for the bandits in Cerro Umbría […]

The above extract is from a death sentence in front of a firing squad, signed in Madrid in 1940, a year after the end of the Civil War.[34]

Analysis

Such documents, death sentences from the Minutes of war councils, have been made public lately, which is important for several reasons. It makes our immediate history visible and, therefore, makes us aware

---

[34] Quoted from: Dulce Chacón, *La voz Dormida,* (Madrid: Alfaguara, 2002), 220-221.

of what happens when dialogue fails. Moreover, it also shows how fragile and worthless human lives had been considered only sixty-six years ago (this sentence was signed in 1939).

The text highlights words such as "rebellion", "death" and "execution", thus establishing a macabre chain of thought and action. But what makes things worse is the fact that the condemned had committed no further crime than choosing to belong to a political party, had demonstrated in the streets and procured food for their comrades. If we analyse such texts devoid of their context we can make our students aware of the lack of logic that links one set of actions with the punishment they are considered by some to deserve. When we add the historical context to the analysis, the cultural and moral disruption a war brings is made all the more evident. Human communities choose to live in democracies because they want freedom: freedom of thought, freedom of action, and freedom to choose one's friends and colleagues. Once these priorities are established, people adhere to them to maintain a sense of belonging. These basic principles are precisely the ones that become deadly dangerous when a war breaks out.

Women are in an even worse situation. In the first place, they have been rarely free to choose friends or affiliations, which, paradoxically, was easier for them during war times. But, no sooner do they achieve some human rights, when these are taken from them. Not only do they partake in the same shortcomings, but they are, in times of war, inextricably linked to their family ties, so that they are made to suffer and are even killed for no other reason than that they are related to men who flew from the enemy or disappeared altogether. Pondering over these documents, students make all kinds of connections, especially students who have either a first-hand memory of similar episodes, or have heard of such from relatives. A death sentence brought to effect (and on multiple occasions) can make history shockingly alive.

4. *Labour Contract – Official Documents*
María Suárez Lafuente

Illustration: Female teachers at the courtyard
(Historical Museum, Blagoevgrad)

Document

The following is agreed upon by, on the one hand, Miss ....,
and on the other the Council of Education of .... School. Miss
.... will start teaching for a period of eight months from
September 1923. The Council of Education will pay her ....
pesetas a month.

Miss .... agrees to the following rules:

Not to get married. If she marries, this contract will be automatically
annulled.
Not to go around with men.
Be at home between 20:00 pm and 6:00 am, unless she is required to
attend in some educational activity.
Not to linger in the ice cafés in the city.
Not to leave the city under any circumstances without a written
permission from the Council of Delegates.

Not to smoke cigarettes. If the teacher were to be surprised smoking, this contract will be automatically annulled.

Not to drink beer, wine nor whisky. If the teacher were to be surprised drinking beer, wine or whisky, this contract will be automatically annulled.

Not to travel in private transport, unless the coach or car is driven by her father or her brother.

Not to wear bright coloured clothes.

Not to dye her hair.

Use at least two petticoats.

Not to wear skirts shorter than five centimetres from her ankles.

Not to use face powder, nor make up nor lipstick.

Keep the classroom clean.

Sweep the floor at least once a day.

Scrub the floor with hot water at least once a week.

Clean the blackboard at least once a day.

Light the fire at 7:00 am so that the room is warm by 8:00, when the children arrive.

Analysis

This text is important for several reasons; in the first place, because it is a contract for female teachers, and completely different from the contract given to male teachers at the same time, and because it is not concerned with the teaching itself, not even with the teacher's set of morals, but is exclusively about the external aspects of both.

It also shows that women were considered eternally under-age creatures, always in need of a man to take care of them (rule 8), but also dangerous for men, as in rule 2. It is important to notice that the so-called rules are, rather, commands, as they are given in a negative form, as if they were the Ten Commandments. They cripple the individual rights of every female teacher to such an extent that they can be called a 'humiliation' inflicted upon the female teaching body, especially so since there was no choice, one either signed the contract or found another kind of employment.

Since teaching was one of the very scarce occupations women could fulfil at the beginning of the century, this text is a good example of the slavery-like situation that women had to endure at the time. However, there are plenty of novels, within the history of Spanish contemporary literature, where women authors fictionalise their own experiences as teachers, and they all agree that being a teacher was a good deal better than being penniless at home, directly under the power and designs of either a father or an unwilling brother.

Many such novels carry telling titles like *Memoirs of a Teacher*, *The Diary of a Teacher* and the like, and most of them were published up to the 1960s. In 1998, Marina Mayoral wrote "In the Parks at Night...", a wonderfully structured short story, based on the archetype of the good primary school teacher, as defined in the contract above. This teacher, while preserving her character socially, to the point of being considered "the angel of the school", leads a double-life of international crime, fooling not only the people in her village, but us readers, right up to the last paragraph. This kind of subversive literature is very effective nowadays in deconstructing social archetypes.

Objects

5. *A Photograph*
Andrea Pető

Illustration: Photo of Eugénia Miskolczy (Ms. Meller)
(personal archive)

Importance

The history of women's activism is the subject of different kinds of forgetting. This is especially true in countries with state-dominated periods, during which women's associations were banned, not only because of the hegemonic rule of the Communist Party, but also because of a class-based feminism in which the middle class and intellectuals were thought to be in need of regulation. The memory of the Holocaust is one such taboo topic and, thus, a subject of forgetting for those female activists who were feminist and Jewish.

Background

Eugénia Miskolczy was born on 14 January 1872 into a Jewish family. Her father was Adolf Mickolczy, a craftsman born on 12 June 1839 in Hódmezővásárhely. Her mother, Laura Weiss, was born on 5 July 1849 in Buda. Her brother József died in 1876, at the age of 6, and her sister Irén died in 1879, at the age of 5. A fourth child was born in 1879. Laura Weiss died of tuberculosis in 1883, when Eugénia was 11.

Eugénia did have a private education, concentrating on languages and music. In 1870, in Buda, she married Artúr Meller who worked as an inspector at the National Bank of Hungary. They had four children: Vilmos was born in 1896, Laura in 1898, Erzsébet in 1899, and Rózsa in 1901. The family lived at 49 Bajcsy-Zsilinszky Street (as it is called today). In 1920 the family converted to the Lutheran faith.

Eugénia was one of the founders of the Feminist Association in 1904 and was a member of its Political Committee. She published articles in the journal *Nő és Társadalom* (Woman and Society), and was a very good public speaker, holding lectures in the Óbuda Democratic Circle, in Szeged and in Transylvania. She was one of the organisers of the 7th Word Congress of the International Women's Suffrage Alliance held in Budapest in 1913, and presented a lecture on women's issues at the Society of Social Sciences (*Társadalomtudományi Társaság*) in 1915. At the banned feminist conference in 1916, Eugénia gave the 'undelivered speeches' as a form of resistance to the ban. She was a member of the National Council (*Nemzeti Tanács*) in 1918 during the bourgeois revolution, delegated by feminists, and she participated in the Paris Peace Congress in 1926, as a member of the Hungarian delegation. She was also a member of the Social Democratic Party and League Against the Death Penalty, and represented the Feminist Association in International Women's Suffrage Alliance and the League for Peace and Freedom. Eugénia is the author of a pamphlet protesting against the execution of Imre Sallai and Sándor Fürst in 1932.[35]

After the German occupation of Hungary in 1944, Eugénia was arrested, and she disappeared. The President of the Republic honoured her with the Silver Liberty Medal in 1946. Her son, Vilmos, survived the forced labour service, and for her daughter, Laura, who was trained as a doctor and as one of the first female psychoanalysts, Eugénia managed to get an affidavit though her international contacts from the women's movement. Her two other daughters survived the

---

[35] Sallai and Fürst were Leftist journalists who were murdered by the paramilitary troops of the Horthy government. The murderers remained unpunished. Among the protesters were poet, Attila József (1905-1937), and writer, Gyula Illyés (1902-1983).

war in the ghetto of Budapest. Currently, the son of Vilmos lives in Budapest and the son and daughter of Laura live in Australia. The Feminist Association was banned in 1951.

Illustration: Photo of Eugénia Miskolczy (Ms. Meller)
(personal archive)

The Two Photographs

The first photograph is well-known and is the only remaining photo of Eugénia Miskolczy, taken from the publication for the Conference on Women's Suffrage, held in Budapest in 1913. For the occasion the organisational committee published a leaflet about its members with a page-size photo and life story in the working languages of the conference. The same photo was sent to me from Australia where Eugénia's grandson lives. He managed to escape from Hungary in 1938 and he keeps the family archive. The document was an annual admission pass to the popular Palatinus Open-air Pool on Margaret Island in Budapest in 1934. Eugénia must have stored the remaining leaflets at her home, and she cut her photo from there for this very practical reason.

The second photo is taken during the Second World War, probably around thirty years after the first, and shows Eugénia in front of her typewriter, wearing a black dress. Regardless of the fact that she had no formal education, Eugénia was always very conscious about intellectual activity. She always led a puritan and socially responsible lifestyle, even when she was financially well-off. After the

48

death of her husband, Eugénia made her living as a translator until employment was impossible due to the anti-Jewish laws.

To Be Learned
Continuity and discontinuity in the women's movement, internationalism, migration, Holocaust.

Assignment
> ➢ Look for an activist in your country from the same generation as Eugénia.
> ➢ What kind of sources do you use to recover that generation of activists? Use the Internet.
> ➢ Compare the turning points of their lives. What makes the difference and how do the women cope with that?
> ➢ How are these activists remembered in the national historiography?
> ➢ What role does women's activism play to recover their memory?
> ➢ Compare the two representations of the very same woman in the two photographs.

Suggested Reading
Andrea Pető, *Hungarian Women in Politics 1945-1951*. Columbia UP, East European Monographs Series, 2003.

6. *Monument*
María Suárez Lafuente

Illustration: The 'Emigrant's Mother'
(*www.geomundos.com/masde40/kai51/madre-del-emigrante_img_1451.html*)

This monument is placed by the shore of the Cantabric Sea in Gijón, an industrial city on the northern coast of Spain. Gijón was a rural community until the last years of the nineteenth century when industry crept in, attracted by the nearby coal mines and the convenient port, open to the Atlantic and fairly close to France and Great Britain. But, by that time, many boys and men had been seeping through that very same port to Central and South America in search of a better life.

Asturias has always been a land of emigration. There is hardly a family that does not count an emigrant, or several, within living memory. Some of them made their fortune and came back for sporadic visits, leaving behind, when they went back to their host countries, big familiar houses and big, renewed churches. But most of them were lost, either to the sea, to diseases, or, simply, to life. There are many

50

tragic stories of loss and frustrated expectations in this part of the country. So, in the 1960s, authorities decided to memorialise this historical fact and had this monument erected. It is called *Madre del Emigrante* (Emigrant's Mother), and it is a familiar tourist sight for those visiting Gijón.

It could have been a classic statue of a loving, patient mother, suffering quietly the absence of her sons while she goes about her chores in life. That would fit the archetype, not only of the mother, but of the female at large (considered by patriarchy to exist primarily to be a mother). But the artist was not thinking of pleasing the audience. He did get into the feelings of a woman trained to *be a mother*, used to making that function the priority of her life, and then deprived cruelly of it. The 'Emigrant's Mother' is an expressionist monument that challenges any pretension of complacency. That is why it was a very controversial monument for years, because those that would like to sacralise maternity (that is, to put mothers on an altar and leave them there to wither away) are confronted by this desperate, suffering mother.

Gijón is a city well-known for having several contemporary, unaesthetic monuments that do not allow indifference. But what is particular to this statue is that, in spite of it being a classic and figurative monument, it excites all kind of feelings in those who see it. The mother's gaze, lost in the ocean/horizon, as well as her desperation, clearly constitute a denunciation of careless politics and a dark page in the history of our Principality.

The 'geography of art', the touring of monuments in any city, can tell us many things, not only about our past, but also about our present. Women are usually depicted only in the manner of archetypes and, probably worse, of cultural icons, symbols and metaphors. Or, more often than not, they are not to be found anywhere. Specific citizens, with a name and a profession attached to them, are always men. So that one of the first projects we do with students when they first come to our Women's Studies programme is to walk the city with 'gendered' eyes.

7.   Memories of Furniture
Lada Stevanović

Illustration: The photo of a Wasserbank
(personal archive)

The Source

The source that I have chosen as a basis for this paper is a photograph of a piece of kitchen furniture (*Wasserbank* in German), which was a wedding present to my grandparents from my grandfather's parents, and which my grandmother has preserved since the time of her marriage. Photography, as a document of some object of importance, is a source for constructing narrative functions. Its significance might appear either on the intimate level, in which case its value is more symbolic and personal, or on the functional level, as, for example, some crucial object or tool that was used in everyday life enabling the survival of the family. Photography as a source appears as a core around which the narrative is constructed. There are two different ways of gaining information about it: either through the interview with the foremother herself, or by collecting information from different people that have lived in close relation to her. In this paper, a history of the photographed object will be reconstructed on the basis of the autobiographical accounts of its owner, my grandmother, Nada, both through the formal interview, which was recorded, as well as through spontaneous conversations relating to the interview that were not perceived by my grandmother to be part of the interview process.

At first, the *Wasserbank* was functional, but, over time, it lost its practical purpose and was kept as a memento. Particularly interesting is the fact that the piece was moved four times, coinciding with the number of countries that my grandmother has lived in. The story of the *Wasserbank* will sketch the wider political context, and its impact on the personal life of Nada.

The *Wasserbank* was an important piece of kitchen furniture, particularly the bank, which was used for the water bowel and water cans, during a time when there were no water pipes. This *Wasserbank* was made, in my grandmother's words, by the best carpenter in Vikovci, who was German by origin. My grandmother called him *Schwabo*.[36]

The Story

My grandparent's wedding took place in 1940. Nada was from a poor family of four daughters, whose father died unexpectedly. Since her mother was not able to feed the whole family, two daughters had to

---

[36] *Schwabo* is a term that was commonly used for denoting domestic people of German origin. After the Second World War it became a disdainful term, characteristic of all names denoting German people. Life for more than half a million *Folks-Deutschers*, or 'domestic Germans' who lived in the Kingdom of Yugoslavia, became very difficult after the war in the Socialist Federal Republic of Yugoslavia (SFRJ). Although part of the domestic population, because of their national origin, they were identified with the German army and punished – deported, deprived of their possessions, sent to prisoners' camps or assimilated. The only ones who survived were those living in mixed families. Germans were not even acknowledged as a minority in the SFRJ. My grandmother's mother-in-law, whose wedding present was this piece of kitchen furniture, was of German origin.

work, while another continued to go to school. My grandmother was fourteen when she started work in the factory where each shift lasted for ten hours. At the age of seventeen, she married Mato, the young and wealthy owner of a jewellery store, who had just returned from two years army service in the Kingdom of Yugoslavia. This is where the story of the *Wasserbank* begins. After one year of calm and peaceful life, the war broke out. The NDH (Independent State of Croatia) was established, and Mato was mobilised as *domobran* to serve in its army as a translator. The daughter of the young couple was about to be born. After the breakdown of the NDH, my grandfather came back home.

"But then there was occupation again."

It was with these words that my grandmother described the German occupation and the arrival of the liberating partisan army. This statement was one of the rare moments in which she made a clear statement against the communist regime, even though at this moment such a statement would fit into the dominant political climate of Croatia. However, later, in one of our conversations, my grandmother said that actually it was much more peaceful in the period of the NDH during the Second World War than when the partisans came. She said that many women were raped and a lot of them robbed and there was extortion all around. However, she imputed such behaviour exclusively to Russian partisans.

My grandfather was denunciated by some neighbour and taken away to be executed by the partisan army. Luckily, his life was saved by a Serbian soldier. However, my grandmother did not get any information about Mato for several months. She was going from prison to prison, searching for him and trying to get information about him.

> And I was going from prison to prison. And no one wanted to tell me anything. They were asking if he was German or Ustaša. And they were calling me by horrible names. And I told them horrible things. You know, I didn't know that it was dangerous to talk like that. And I asked them why the army were taking away decent and honourable men. I told them a lot of horrible things...And one day a man came bringing his wedding ring and clock. And I started to

cry…and my daughter came, she was only three years old, and said, 'Don't cry, daddy will come back.' And that man told me not to cry, Mato was hidden in some cellar in Vinkovci.

Soon after that, in 1944, Mato was mobilised to serve in the partisan army. It was during that time, that representatives of the new establishment – actually a neighbour – gave an order to deprive my grandparents of all of their possessions, except for the house.

Since Mato was a jeweller, I buried a box of gold in the garden. And when the NDH fell apart and I thought that the war had ended, I dug it out. Can you imagine what happened the next day? They came and took everything from us. And I told Mato that I knew who took it… It was Carić, from Vinkovci, assistant in the bookstore. The suitcase opened when they were leaving and watches fell on to the street, and children were running and collecting them. And Mato told me: 'Never mind. It's important that I can buy a hat – the head is here'. But actually, he had changed a lot. He was ruined.

The period after the Second World War was not easy for the family. In the new communist regime, the family became despised and humiliated. My grandmother decided to move to Zagreb, but my grandfather was not in agreement.

I told him that he had promised me that we would live in Zagreb, so I decided to sell the house. He stayed in Vinkovci and I came with two children to Zagreb – our own and a child of my sister's who was like my own son. First we rented a room, while I was looking for a land to buy and a shop to rent for him. One day he came. I asked: 'You came to visit us?' 'No', he said, 'I came to take you away from here.' And I replied: 'I wouldn't go if I were dead! To go back….Everybody would laugh at me! To go back, after all humiliations… Never! And then, he told me that I have to go back. And I replied that I do not have to do it. And he asked me how I would live. I answered that it was my problem. And, of course, he did not go. He stayed. And I found a very nice store for him and nice building-site for us.

They started building the house in 1953. Mato was working hard as a watchmaker, and Nada was building the house, together with the workers.

And so, we began to build. Mato did not interfere. He just told the workers to listen to me. And I was taking care of everything, supervising the construction and working. Every morning I got up at 5 o'clock. I was buying and picking up cement, loading and carrying it on my own. And during that time I did not have a car. I was making drainage, digging, I was even building when some workers had to go home earlier. And I grounded all wall sockets on my own. Once a friend of Mato's came to visit us – he asked me if Mr or Ms Štefanovski were at home. He did not recognise me and did not suppose that I would work on the house like that – I had some ugly scarf on my head and ragged trousers. And then I decided to pretend that I was someone else and told him to come in the afternoon. Then I dressed up nicely and we all had coffee together.

They moved to a new house that was not yet finished. Apart from the oak furniture they brought from Vinkovci, there was the small *Wasserbank* in the new house, the only piece of their old kitchen they had not sold. The new house had water pipes and, so, it did not have a function anymore, and there was no place for it in the kitchen. Not wanting to throw it away, Nada decided to put it by the stairs that lead to the attic, hidden from everyday sight.

By the time they both had grown old, the house was finished and my grandfather was on a pension. Their daughter, my mother, was living in the nearby capital of the Socialist Federal Republic of Yugoslavia (SFRJ), Belgrade. The war began and the SFRJ broke down. This time the family became split, not only by living in two different cities, but also with the state border and the war. My grandmother was an optimist and was full of strength to face any difficulties, but my grandfather had a heart attack. Even though she herself was not young and healthy anymore, she took care of Mato and her mother, who was also very old and very ill. First, her mother died in 1992 and, then, a year later, Mato followed. Contacts with the family in Belgrade were difficult. We could not see each other as often as before, nor could we talk on the 'phone, because direct telephone connections did not exist. The house was too big, expensive, and empty to live there alone and, so, my grandmother decided to sell the house and move to a smaller flat. Of course, not everything could be moved and many things were thrown away. But the *Wasserbank* was renovated and exhibited in the kitchen, side-by-side with the modern facilities.

Conclusions

This paper illustrates how photography can be used as a framework around which a narrative about a foremother's life can be constructed based on a personal interview with her. Another option for constructing such a narrative in relation to photography, is to interview different people close to the owner of the object, who personally know the foremother, as well as the photographed object. As is the case in the narrative about my grandmother's life, I had the opportunity to spend quite a long time on this research and to try both options before deciding on the one that I found to be more fruitful, informative and useful. Although in the interview we were constantly turning to the object in the photograph and its history, it was inevitable that we also talked about my grandmother's life before marriage, as well as about the traumatic first years of marriage when her husband was away from home. Thus, what I would conclude from this interview is that photography can be used as a motive for conversation, moving it sometimes in unexpected directions, and exceeding the initial topic. However, even though recollections sometimes seemed far and disconnected at first, they all came together to constitute a complete narrative, which was, after all, the aim of the research.

The advantage of this method of constructing a narrative around a photographed object appears to be a kind of accessory, but it is also a controlling instrument that directs the interview. At this point, the question arises about my own objectivity as an interviewer. First of all, I have known a lot of stories from before, which might have given me the opportunity to direct the conversation in the way I wanted. However, the defined topic and a fixation upon the object in the photograph prevented me from doing so and, actually, it turned out that I heard a lot of the stories for the first time. So, the final result was that I did not hear what I had expected, which I certainly regard as beneficial.

Furthermore, since the interviewee was my own grandmother, I had the opportunity for a lot of spontaneous conversations that were not perceived by my grandmother as related to the interview. This was our usual communication to which I turned more attention, sometimes casually asking questions related to our interview (a kind of indirect metalinguistic 'talk about talk'). The tone of informal conversation was quite different from the formal tone in the recorded interview. Besides, my grandmother revealed her own feelings much more freely in those chats.[37] The advantage of informal conversation not only lies in its spontaneity, but also in its suitability for a female socio-communication, as it is understood by Kristina Minister. According to her, the form of oral history interviews has been developed in a male socio-communication system for which 'taking the floor' is characteristic, while women's communication is based more on the exchange of personal and affiliative issues. Interviewing women successfully would, therefore, require some kind of adaptation to a female communicational context.[38]

The photograph of the *Wasserbank* represents memory that has been kept through all of my grandmother's moves from one place to another. However, each move can be related, directly or indirectly, to a change of a certain regime/state. My grandmother is the one who initiated the family's migration from a small town to a bigger one in order to run away from provincial surroundings, and in order to adapt better to new circumstances. Although she has lived as a house-wife, only dealing with issues related to the running of a household (although, in her case, this included the building of a house), she has never bowed to anyone's authority. Her resolute and decisive attitude

---

[37] However, in this situation I faced the moral dilemma of revealing what my grandmother told me in confidence and whether it is something that she would agree to be made public.

[38] Minister researches different forms of socio-communicational codes and situations in which women and men act differently. For example, men are more adapted to speaking in public and in monologues, unlike women who communicate easier together with other women, preferring to take turns in conversation while somebody else is speaking, and developing, by reference, from the previous speaker. For more on this topic, see Kristina Minister, "A Feminist Frame of the Oral History Interview," in Sherna Berger Gluck and Daphne Patai (eds.), *Women's Words: The Feminist Practice of Oral History Interview*, (Routledge, 1991), 27-41.

towards her husband might also be explained by his under-privileged position in the communist regime. What I find most interesting and precious about my grandmother's life is the complex ambiguity towards the different regimes she has lived under. She claims that the most difficult period of her life was childhood, not only because of poverty, but because of the humiliation that she experienced.[39] Although marriage changed her status for the better, it actually did not last for long and she was stigmatised again – this time as an ex-bourgeois. Although the family was deprived by communists of almost all its property under the SFRJ (my grandmother's term for the partisans coming to Vinkovci is 'occupation'), she has always regarded socialism as more fair and humane than capitalism. The last war, the decomposition of the SFRJ, and the new difficulties related to it, made the lifestyle that had vanished, and her life in it, even more appreciated.

The object in the photograph, as well as its history as re-told in the interview, function as a skeleton for reconstructing the metaphoric flesh of my grandmother's life. Regime and country changes, with their impact on her destiny, appear in her life as complex ambiguities and contradictions that I have tried to sketch out in this narrative reconstruction, most probably roughly and failing to preserve finer nuances.

---

[39] She told me about the rudeness of the owner of the sewing factory in which she worked, as well as about the rudeness of the doctor in the hospital where she was operated on. After the operation, nurses brought her to sew some sheets. However, she made friends with an older, rich lady who protected her.

8. *A Birthday Card from My Family Archive*
Leena Kurvet-Käosaar

Illustration: A birthday card given by Helga Valgerist-Sitska to her granddaughter Leena Käosaar for her 18th birthday on 22 November, 1987. Painted by Helga Valgerist-Sitska, the poem inside by Katre Ligi, a female Estonian poet.

Description

Last year, when I was organising some old papers at my mother's place, I found a birthday card my maternal grandmother, Helga Valgerist-Sitska, had given me for my 18th birthday. It is not an ordinary card one might buy from a stationery store or a post office, but one she had painted herself. My grandmother was the most important and influential person in my life during my formative years, and the card is her message to me upon my coming of age. It can be looked upon as a document in our family archive, which lays scattered around in my childhood home and consists of photos, letters, official documents from various time periods, Christmas and birthday cards, diaries of some family members, and newspaper clippings, amongst other things. The card's full meaning can be grasped only when accompanied by my grandmother's life story that highlights subversive female practices directed against a totalitarian regime.

In the centre of the card there is a young woman, surrounded by four other women of various ages looking at her. Below is a flower, freshly bloomed, and in the background are blue skies studded with light white clouds. The young woman's face looks contemplative and self-absorbed in a confident kind of way. Inside the card is a poem by an Estonian female poet, Katre Ligi. The poem talks about "the lure of the school of life," of wanting and needing to go nowhere special, with no definite plans in mind but, rather, an inner need simply to wander along, to touch "icy sun and hot snow." The author, Katre Ligi, is better known as the wife of a major contemporary Estonian poet, Hando Runnel, famous for his semi-dissident poems especially in the 1970s and '80s. I think that my grandmother's selection of a poem by a fine female poet, whose talent has, to a certain extent, always been overshadowed by her famous husband, is not accidental.

Background

In order to show the full implications of the card, I will provide a brief overview of my grandmother's life. Born in 1914, she studied Law at Tartu University in the 1930s, at a time when women formed a small minority among university students and an even smaller minority among Law students. She graduated during the first years of the Second World War and was in the job market at the time of the Soviet occupation of Estonia. She married my grandfather, almost ten years her elder, during her university years, and gave birth to three children. My mother was the second child and the only daughter. Although she was certainly aware that not much was left of the code of law of the independent republic of Estonia by that time, the fact that she was turned down, as politically unsuitable, for every job, including that of a junior assistant in a chemistry lab, must have been quite difficult to accept. Well-read in many subjects and fluent in three foreign languages, she was in her forties before she was able to find her first professional job as a legal councillor of cooperative housing projects at Tartu municipal government. As the job offered little professional challenge, she retired in her early sixties and stayed at home to take care of my younger sister and me.

Looking back on her life, I am convinced that my grandmother's decision to retire from public life and dedicate herself to raising us must have been a very conscious one. However, it was certainly not solely triggered by a woman's sense of duty to her children and grandchildren, nor because she felt that a woman's place was (only) at home. Rather, she must have decided that, given the political regime, she would never be able to have the career she had dreamt of, that of a legal councillor in the civil service.

Although my childhood, during the 1970s and '80s, coincided with what is known as Estonia's 'stagnation period', it is possible that my grandmother never ceased to believe that times would change and that Estonia would regain independence. She died in April 1989, at the height of the so-called 'Singing Revolution' that culminated in the re-establishment of independent statehood for Estonia in August 1991. It must have been her firm belief that keeping the spirit of independence alive at home, and devoting herself to educating us in the best way she could, would be the most valuable contribution to her country and to her family.

We lived at her beautiful capacious apartment with furniture and ceramic chandeliers designed by my grandfather, paintings by well-known Estonian artists, and shelves of books running along almost all the walls in all the rooms. My grandmother cooked (I still use many of her recipes), kept the house clean, and did many other household chores, including the endless queuing that was an inseparable part of everyday life during Soviet times. More importantly, however, she educated us, weaving practical knowledge and the management of daily problems with philosophical issues, and providing us with extra knowledge on almost every subject we learned at school. For history, this meant telling us a different story altogether, one of the years of national independence in Estonia and of the Soviet occupation and repressions that followed. This was a story that would have been dangerous for me to flaunt, but my grandmother trusted me with it nonetheless, counting on me to know how to handle this information.

It is no exaggeration to say that much of what I learned during my schools years my grandmother taught me, in one way or another. As a result of her guidance, neither I nor my sister ever doubted that we would go to university after high school and then realise our professional potential; we simply took it for granted. When growing up, I was hardly aware that the traditional course of life would be much different for men and women. My grandmother taught us to think independently, and to educate ourselves in many different fields, thus preparing us fully to realise ourselves professionally in adulthood. She also provided us with the capacity to look at life from different points of view, to take time to gain a perspective, to contemplate, and to always retain an inquisitive stance.

In outlining how the New Historicist understanding of history allows her to "bring the texts of women's personal writing and the private worlds they describe into the marketplace of public culture",[40] Helen Buss encourages us to search for a "fuller reading of female discourses"[41] that "will yield contextual truths that reveal the places of women in culture and history and the many possibilities of female subjectivity that will revise male models of truth and human nature."[42]

Challenging the position of traditional history, which attributes all the weight of history to the public sphere dominated by men, Tiina Kirss underlines the importance and depth of the frequently undervalued private sphere into which the majority of women's experience falls: "the research done in women's history over the past few decades, based on 'more personal kinds of documents of lesser importance', has shown how rich, multifunctional and intricate the private sphere can really be."[43] Kirss also emphasises that it is in the private sphere where "the network of communal traditions and customs as well as language is passed from generation to generation"[44] that makes women and the private sphere they represent the "most immediate and important embodiment of a nation's memory".[45]

---

[40] Helen Buss, "A Feminist Review of New Historicism to Give Fuller Readings of Women's Private Writings," in Suzanne L. Bunkers and Cynthia A. Huff (eds.), *Inscribing the Daily. Critical Essays on Women's Diaries*. (Amherst: U of Massachusetts Press, 1996), 86-103, 222.

[41] *ibid.*, 225.

[42] *ibid.*

[43] Tiina Kriss, "Ariadne lõngakera: Eesti naiste Siberilood nende elulugudes," (Ariadne's Clew: Deportation Experience in the Life Stories of Estonian Women) in *Paar sammukest 16: Eesti Kirjandusmuuseumi aastaraamat* (Yearbook of the Estonian Literary Museum, 1999), 23-31.

[44] *ibid*, 24.

[45] *ibid.*

My grandmother's efforts in raising us in an intellectually stimulating environment where national values and concerns played a central role during times when knowledge in many fields was highly censored and distorted, effectively functions as a strategy of subtle domestic resistance to the Soviet regime. During most of her adult life, the main focus of her life was the private sphere – her home, her children and grandchildren. Under the Soviet regime, her professional career was cut short before it could even properly begin, and she was never able to realise her full potential professionally, since, for my grandmother, there were strict limits to the extent any collaboration with the Soviet regime was ethically possible. For example, one such limit, which influenced the professional life of both of my grandparents, was their refusal to become members of the Communist Party: my grandmother was never promoted at her job for this reason and my grandfather was fired from his.

My grandmother, however, fulfilled herself through her children and, perhaps more importantly even, her grandchildren, particularly me (born in 1969) and my sister (born in 1975). Combining woman's traditional domestic responsibilities with diverse educational activities, she managed to considerably lessen, albeit in a small circle of people, the power of the Soviet regime to distort knowledge, to erase and modify a nation's memory, and to reduce the people in occupied countries to obedient and silent subjects.

Assignment

> ➢ Can the source be looked upon as a conscious act of a woman who assumes the role of a foremother herself? How?
> ➢ Can you find a document or an object from your family archive that has, at least partially, similar connotations? You can also search local archives (or online archives) accessible to you or use a text or image from a published or otherwise well-known source (e.g. letter, diary extract, journalistic text, painting, cartoon).
> ➢ Explain the context and the connotations to the others, keeping in mind the axes of gender and any of the following: social position, nationality, the relationship between the public and private sphere, political situation.

> Read Helen M. Buss, "A Feminist Review of New Historicism to Give Fuller Readings of Women's Private Writings" (in Suzanne L. Bunkers and Cynthia A. Huff eds., *Inscribing the Daily. Critical Essays on Women's Diaries,* Amherst, U of Massachusetts Press, 1996, 86– 103) and discuss the value of your chosen text/object/image in terms of possible feminist applications of a missing historical conscience.
> What female discourses of your source can you identify? How do they challenge or modify the general (male) models of truth and history?

Texts

9.   *Private Letters*
       Erla Hulda Halldorsdottir

Illustration: Jakobina Jonsdottir (Bína). The photo is not dated but might have been taken while Bína stayed in Reykjavik 1865-1867, where she had high expectations of betterment. The National Museum Collection of Photographs and Prints (Thodminjasafn Islands): Mms. 35849

Introduction

What is the worth of personal sources such as private letters, diaries, memoirs and autobiographies for historical research, dissemination and teaching? I believe they are an inexhaustible and invaluable source of knowledge about the past. They especially, though not exclusively, gain validity in women's history, which has not been part of the official institutional history until the last few decades. Private sources are the course or venue of women's thought and knowledge, and incorporate stories of their daily lives, and record how they experienced joy and sorrow.[46] By using these sources in historical research and writing, scholars not only have the opportunity to enliven history, but also to give a voice to women of the past.[47] People – students, scholars and the interested public – want to learn about personal experiences and daily life in the past, such as feelings, hopes and expectations. These are things to which all human beings can relate. As Pető and Waaldijk have already pointed out, a personal approach to the past, more explicitly, to situate oneself in the place of an individual or a foremother, can enhance the understanding of history and the historical context.[48]

A Window to the Past

The use of private letters in historical research can easily be related to standpoint theory, not least when an extensive collection of letters is used to reconstruct a life or the history of a certain era. Correspondence can be seen as a window to the past through which the researcher looks. She situates herself by the person who wrote the letters and even takes her stand – whether conscious of it or not. Private letters, however, should not be used without critical analysis, since they reflect the opinion and view of an individual and should, therefore, be used carefully in any generalisations. Letters are written in connection with who the recipient is: in other words, the relationship between the writer and the recipient influences what is written about and how. A private letter is usually written with sincerity, nothing is kept back or hidden. But it can also be written in order to deceive any recipient who might see or hear the letter, as it was not uncommon for private letters, or parts of them, to be read aloud to a household. It is clear that those who wrote letters were

---

[46] Personal sources are important not only for women's history but also for history writing in general. Icelandic historians have increasingly used these sources in their research in the last few years, mainly when researching the history of 'ordinary' people.

[47] In this context, see June Purvis, "Using Primary Sources When Researching Women's History from a Feminist Perspective." *Women's History Review*, Vol. 1. No. 2 (1992), 273-306.

[48] Andrea Pető and Berteke Waaldijk, "Writing the Lives of Foremothers, the History and Future of a Feminist Teaching Tool," in *The Making of European Women's Studies*, Vol. IV (Utrecht, 2002), 152.

aware that their letters might become public.[49] Private letters are more than what can be read in them – black on white. It is important to take notice of what is in-between the lines, what is not written, or even hinted at.

I have used private letters in my research on the history of women in the nineteenth century, and they have given me invaluable insight into women's daily lives, as well as their hopes and expectations, self-image and the image of the nineteenth century woman.

Bína

One of the most intriguing women I researched was born at Myvatn in northern Iceland in 1835. She was given the name Karolina Jakobina, but was usually called Bína. She was the daughter of a priest and his wife, the youngest of thirteen surviving brothers and sisters. Her home was rather well-set financially and Bína got a better education than most girls of her time. She learned to write, which many people thought unnecessary for women, and had the leisure to practise the skill, building up a network of correspondence with friends, sisters, brothers and kinswomen. Bína was seventeen years old when she moved with her parents to her brother's home in a *fjord* in eastern Iceland. There, she hoped for some guidance in feminine virtues from her sister-in-law, but, due to the latter's sickness which lasted for years, Bína's education was much less than she had hoped for. Contrary to her dreams and longings it became Bína's lot to take on the domestic duties of her brother's home, in addition to her concern for her parent's welfare.

From 1865 to 1867, Bína stayed in Reykjavik, Iceland's capital, which was hardly more than a small village with nearly two thousand inhabitants. The purpose of Bína's stay there was to give her a chance to improve herself, but her vivid letters, full of descriptions of her 'new' life, also reveal her conscientiousness towards her family and the fact that she sometimes felt as though she wasn't doing anything useful.

---

[49] Swedish historian Eva Helen Ulvros mentions this in her biography on Sophie Elkan, an intimate friend of the writer Selma Lagerlöf. The biography is based on correspondence. See Eva Helen Ulvros, *Sophie Elkan. Hennes liv och vänskapen med Selma Lagerlöf* (Sophie Elkan. Her life and the friendship with Selma Lagerlöf), (Lund, 2001).

Bína socialised with the elite, learned some French, listened to a *pianoforte* for the first time, attended performances and danced on board a French battleship on Napoleon Day, 15 August. But duty called and, before she knew it, her stay came to an end and she had to go back home where she lived until 1870, when she married a well-known politician and poet, Grimur Thomsen. He proposed without having seen her, sending her a letter by mail, and it took Bína almost two years to make up her mind.

A considerable amount of Bína's correspondence has been preserved, both her own letters and those written to her. The letters I find most interesting are from the period between 1850 and 1870, which reveal an impatience and dissatisfaction with her condition. This can be gathered not only from what Bína writes explicitly, but also from what is implied. There is a struggle within her – on the one hand, there is a young, dutiful daughter, who knows what her role in life should be. And, on the other hand, there is the woman who so desperately wants something else, something that is not available for women. This can be seen in the following excerpts:

13 November 1853.[50]

> Even though I am quite happy here, as was expected, it seems as my mind is seeking for something else to dwell on, even though it hardly knows what it is. [...] Kristrun [the sister in law] wishes me all the best she can but I do not know if there is any chance here for betterment for me, there is so much to do and worry about in this world.

12 January 1857

> How unhappy I am always being portioning and dealing with the servants, who have become so ungrateful and aggressive with their Masters. As a matter of fact I can restrain myself talking to them, but it makes me rather unhappy that it became my calling – which I have never been keen on, to have a woman's work; but it would make me happy if it would be useful for someone.

---

[50] All the excerpts are taken from letters that Bína wrote to her sister, Solveig Jonsdottir. The letters are preserved in the manuscript department at the National and University Library in Reykjavik: *Lbs* 2748 4to.

14 January 1860

>Kristrun is always feeling better and better [...] but still she does not take any [duty] from me yet, I am though hoping that if her recovery continues, she could possibly take over in the spring, with the help of her daughters, who now have become efficient girls, though are still unused to it [running a household]; I would be happy to be able to do something else.

25 September 1860

>[…] most of all I have wanted to learn something good and useful, but that desire has vanished, because what little I know on household business and studying I've learned from what I've noticed, from what I have heard and seen, not that I have been taught.

20 September 1863

>[...] write me now [...] something about the parliamentarian[51] even though I do not understand politics. Many of those who have knowledge [in politics] say that he talks daringly in parliament and that the country has a good son in him. There is need for such a man because there aren't so many and it shall also make me happy even though I am only a daughter. Had I been a boy, I would most likely have been a parliamentarian, but then I would have had to be a little bit more of a speaker.

18 November 1869

>It has often come to my mind to wish if I could ease the weight on your shoulder, which is more than mine, or if I would be able to help you with the children, even though it wouldn't be for more than 1 winter, but there has always been something which has got in the way [...] up to this time mainly the reason that girls such as I are always more of a burden than help.

---

[51] Bína's brother-in-law, who was a politician and a member of Althing (parliament).

Analysis

What do those excerpts tell us and how can we use them to shed light on women's history, on history in broader contexts, and how can they be used to compare with other women, other countries and cultures? The excerpts clearly show the longings of a young girl and a woman. Her financial and social status is good, at least when compared with most Icelandic women at that time. All the same, something disturbs her, something she finds difficult to define. Apparently, it is the traditional role of women, or the space she was given as a woman, that is restricting for Bína. She desired what she calls 'betterment', meaning education: to learn something useful and practical. Before 1874 there was no formal educational institution for women in Iceland. Apart from being a maid, no professions or jobs were available for women who could not or did not want to get married. Women's talents and desire for education could not be fulfilled. That was the opinion of one of Bína's brothers when he, in a letter to her, wrote about her talent for studying: "[you] should have been a boy in trousers then you would have been more able to resign to it."[52] Bína did picture herself as a man when writing about her interest in politics and in asking for news on her brother-in-law, and wrote that she would "most likely" have been a parliamentarian if she had been born a boy.

This re-gendering or masculinisation of women can be seen in private letters and also in the memoirs and autobiographies of Icelandic women of that generation (born before and around 1850). They did not doubt the different roles of men and women, considering them to be natural and normal, and could not imagine that they, as women, could intrude in 'manly' professions. In order to imagine otherwise, they had to envision themselves as men. Nevertheless, they struggled and even expressed their discontent, as Bína did, as she tried to find a way to liberate herself from the restrictions of habits and practice.

Bína's correspondence provides an opportunity to explore and discuss the boundaries between public and private life, and how they were defined. It makes one wonder if they differed according to status and class and what opportunities women had to cross boundaries of

---

[52] Sigfus Jonsson to Jakobina Jonsdottir, 10 July 1866 (National and University Library, Lbs 3180 4to).

gender. To what extent was society flexible? Where were women allowed to enter the public sphere and where not?[53] In that context, the researcher must bear in mind the institutions that were most influential in the preservation and continuous reproduction of gender roles: the state, family, the educational system, and the church.[54]

Correspondence, such as Bína's provides room for exploring the image of women in the period in question and women's image of themselves, evident in the last quotation from Bína's letters where she expresses her wish to help her sister. For many reasons she had no opportunity to do that, but, according to Bína, the main reason was that girls like her were "more of a burden than help". Bína had at last realised that it created trouble to think too much and want too much, to do something beyond the possible, as she had done for years.[55] By the time Bína was 34 years old, she still had not answered the proposal of marriage from almost a year earlier. She did not know the man except by reputation and was not willing to accept him unless she knew if "any opinion is the same".[56] Bína knew that the only realistic option was to marry, since only then would she become a 'real' woman just like her contemporaries in the nineteenth century were expected to be.[57]

Foremothers and Different Cultures

Without doubt, Bína's correspondence – and life – is very useful in the Icelandic context where it can be used to shed light on the general status of women, and to explore their rights and different

---

[53] See Leonore Davidoff, Catherine Hall, *Family Fortunes. Men and Women of the English Middle Class 1780-1890* (1987). The revised edition from 2002 is recommended because of the new introduction by Davidoff and Hall. See also Jane Rendall, "Women and the Public Sphere." *Gender and History*, Vol. 11. No. 3., (1999), 475-488.

[54] Pierre Bourdieu, *Masculine Domination*, (Oxford, 2001), 85.

[55] In my sources (autobiographies and private letters) I have come across comments where women write that they almost regret what little they have studied, mainly at the women's schools. Their reason is that this study has opened a small window to a world they have no chance to participate in, therefore, it is possibly better to live in happy ignorance!

[56] Jakobina Jonsdottir to Thora Petursdottir Thoroddsen 8 Aug. 1869, (The National Museum, 192).

[57] In Bína's correspondence to her sister, Solveig, we can see very clearly how conscious she is about their different roles in life. It is obvious that Bína finds her life (at least until her marriage) less worthy than her sister's, who is a mother, housewife and wife. Even though Bína did act as housewife at her brother's home, it was always as a substitute, something she did willingly and unwillingly.

opportunities for education and betterment from various perspectives. Bína's life would also be useful in a foremother project for comparison with other women.

In the European context, Icelandic society differs in many ways from others. The small size of the nation and the geographic isolation of the country created a rather monotonous society where most people lived in the countryside and urbanisation was primarily in the shape of very small fishing villages. But this does, in fact, provide opportunities for interesting comparisons by allowing the student/researcher to consider differences between geographical locations.

Assignment

- ➢ Did Bína have something in common with women in Ireland, Denmark, Hungary or Greece?
- ➢ What were the civil and political rights of these women?
- ➢ Is there something in common in their writings or in their lives?
- ➢ How did they express their expectations? What differences are there?
- ➢ What is the role of different cultures, religions and constitutions?
- ➢ For a student in a foremother project or a seminar on women's history it can be rewarding and exciting to consider if the foremother, grandmother or great-grandmother had something in common with a woman in Iceland or in any other distant country, even more common than with, for example, upper class women in her own country?
- ➢ Is there some identity that goes beyond countries, cultures and continents without trying to mould every woman in the same form?

It is necessary to put a woman's life – the biography or the biographical fragment the student or researcher has put together from correspondence, memoirs, narratives or diaries – in context to the grand narrative, the official history of the nation/country, and ask how a particular woman's (foremother's) life fits into the official history.[58] The small must be compared to the big, the unique or particular to the general, and the coherence between the social order and the individual must be explored.

> ➢ To what extent did the individual influence his/her surroundings and to what extent does the society constrain the individual?
> ➢ What is the interaction of society and the individual?[59]

Correspondence of the past can be used in research, teaching (and the dissemination of history in the wider context) and, thereby, may give the history of countries, nations and continents a more profound meaning. Correspondence can be used as one of many sources when trying to describe past times, and it can be the main source in a narrative (biography) of an individual's life that can be reflected in the society s/he lives in. Seen from my standpoint, private letters are one of the most important sources on the lives of nineteenth century women, their thoughts and activities, both for the purpose of historical research and for that of teaching women's history.

---

[58] See the discussion on the possibilities of the foremother project in: Andrea Pető and Berteke Waaldijk, "Writing the Lives of Foremothers. History and Future of a Feminist Teaching Tool," in Rosi Braidotti, Janny Niebert and Sanne Hirs, (eds.), *The Making of European Women's Studies* Vol. IV (Utrecht, 2002), 149-162; and "Memories, Histories and Narratives," in Rosi Braidotti, Edyta Just and Marlise Mensink, (eds.), *The Making of European Women's Studies* Vol. V (Utrecht, 2004), 173-176.

[59] Gro Hagemann, *Moderne og postmoderne.' Feminisme og historieskrivning. Inntrykk fra en reise,* ('Modern and Postmodern.' Feminism and the Writing of History. The Influence of a Journey), (Oslo, 2003).

10. The Books She Reads. Novels for Girls as a Source for Women's Life Stories.[60]
Berteke Waaldijk

Illustration: Books by Anne Frank and by Cissy van Marxveldt
(Photograph Peter Romijn)

Background

> Towards the end of the eighteenth century a change came about which, if I were rewriting history, I should describe more fully and think of greater importance than the Crusades or the Wars of the Roses. The middle class women began to write. (Virginia Woolf, *A Room of One's Own*)[61]

It is often possible to find out what novels a woman read in her youth. Diaries, letters, oral communication, or the remnants of her library

---

[60] The following article contains excerpts from my article "Reading Anne Frank as a Woman." *Women's Studies International Forum,* 16.4 (1993) 327-335. Permission by Elsevier Science Ltd. has been requested.
[61] Virginia Woolf, *A Room of One's Own* [1929] (London: Grafton Books, 1988), 62.

with books that contain her name may point the researcher to novels that have inspired, amused, taught or shocked the foremother whose life is being studied. These novels can be a source of knowledge about the way she may have experienced her life. Reading the same text as a foremother has read in her youth offers the student/scholar an opportunity to compare her own reading experience with that of the foremother, and it can lead to reflection on the way fictional narratives may have played a role in the fashioning of the self and the stories about this woman.

Since the rise of the novel at the end of the eighteenth century, writing and reading novels has had to do with class, with gender and with the cult of domesticity. As the quotation from Virginia Woolf indicates, middle class women in the nineteenth and twentieth centuries have written novels, and they have read many. Nancy Armstrong, who quotes Woolf, argues that novels helped to create and form the private sphere and the locations where the 'self', in the Foucauldian sense, was developed. Reading a novel has been seen as a good pastime for women who were supposed to remain in the domestic sphere. Novels directed at women described themes and problems from the private sphere: the search for matrimony, motherhood, lost children, lost families, and, of course, love and happiness ever after. Within Modernism, novels written and read by women became the object of derision in literary criticism.[62] They were ridiculed as cheap, sentimental, and lacking literary quality.[63] However, novels that were read by women form a rich source of knowledge about women's lives.

When one studies the life of a woman in the past, it is, therefore, useful to ask about her reading habits. The books she has read, and especially the books that she liked, can shed light on her ambitions, on the way she saw herself, and on the cultural capital available to her.[64] Because most novels from the past are still around and available for

[62] Nancy Armstrong, *Desire and Domestic Fiction. A Political History of the Novel*, (Oxford UP, 1987).

[63] Sandra M. Gilbert and Susan Gubar, *No Man's Land: The Place of the Woman Writer in the Twentieth Century*, (Yale UP, 1988). For a critique of late-twentieth century ideas about women reading 'cheap novels' see Janice A. Radway, *Reading the Romance: Women, Patriarchy, and Popular Literature*, (U of North Carolina Press, 1984).

[64] For the concept of cultural capital, see Pierre Bourdieu, *Distinction: A Social Critique of the Judgement of Taste* (Routledge & Kegan Paul, 1986).

reading, the student/scholar of a woman's life can actually read what the foremother has read. This may allow a 're-enactment' of an experience of the foremother, and will offer the opportunity to reflect on resemblances and differences between the student and her foremother. In addition, a novel, as a story about experiences, offers an invitation to think about the narrative structure of the student's story about her foremother.

A Novel for Girls: An Author Admired by Anne Frank

I will illustrate these points with the example of a Dutch novel for girls, which was read by Anne Frank during her and her family's time in hiding from Nazi persecution.[65] *The Diary of Anne Frank* is the testimony of a young Jewish girl in Amsterdam during the German occupation of the Netherlands. Anne Frank's family went into hiding to escape deportation to the Nazi death camps, but, in the summer of 1944, the hiding place was discovered, and Anne and her family were deported. Anne died, and only her father survived the war, after which he published his daughter's diary, now a world-famous text about the experience of persecution during the Holocaust, with many reprints and translations.

The *Diary* can be read in many ways. In the following paper I will show how a detailed study of a novel that Anne Frank loved can shed new light on *The Diary of Anne Frank*, and on how Anne imagined herself and her writing. In her D*iary*, Anne Frank writes several times about how much she liked the books of Cissy van Marxveldt. She especially liked the four volumes of the *Joop ter Heul* series, about a young girl, 'Joop', who went to school, got married and became a mother.[66] Van Marxveldt was not exactly part of the Dutch literary canon, but many girls, from the 1920s until the 1980s, were familiar with her work, which can best be described as comic novels for girls and young female adults. They humorously describe the lives of girls at school, during courtship, and in the early phases of marriage.

---

[65] The following is an excerpt from my article "Reading Anne Frank as a Woman." *Women's Studies International Forum*, 16.4 (1993), 327-335.

[66] Cissy van Marxvelt, *Joop ter Heul*. The novel was printed and reprinted from 1919 until the end of the twentieth century. No English translation exists.

In *The Diary of Anne Frank* one can easily determine the date of Anne's reading *Joop ter Heul:* an entry in version *a*[67], dated 22 September, 1942, reads: "I've finished *Joop ter Heul* so quickly that I am not allowed new books till next Saturday." The day before this entry, Anne referred to the novel for the first time. So we can assume that Anne must have read *Joop ter Heul* somewhere in the third week of September 1942. Like so many girls of her generation, Anne took an immediate liking to Cissy van Marxveldt's style. Remarkably, from this point until December 1942, Anne wrote almost all her diary entries in the form of letters to one of the characters from the *Joop ter Heul* books, although the letters are addressed to the heroine's friends, never to Joop herself. In these letters, Anne chronicles life in the secret annexe where her family lived in hiding, as well as aspects of her daily life. But, more often than not, she also included references to events in the lives of these fictional friends. For example, on 14 October, 1942, Anne sent greetings to an addressee's fiancé. Writing to 'Pien', a newly-wed friend, she asks whether, after the first days of the honeymoon, there are "signs of fertilization" yet, continuing her letter with a story about real friends expecting a baby. Needless to say, Cissy van Marxveldt never discussed pregnancy openly in her books.

From the third week in September 1942, Anne's diary entries, in version *a*, were much more regular than during the first two months. We do not know how long Anne Frank continued to write to the fictional characters because version *a* is incomplete: entries from December 1942 until December 1943 are missing. From December 1943, Anne wrote all her entries in the form of letters to 'Kitty'. At some point, between December 1942 and December 1943, she must have decided that this was going to be the form that she would use.

---

[67] In this paper I refer to the critical edition of the diaries of Anne Frank, published in 1986. This edition contains version *a* (the first version of the diary as written by Anne Frank between summer 1941 and summer 1944); version *b*, a revised version of her diary (re-written by Anne Frank in the spring and the summer of 1944 with an eye on publication of her diary after the war); and version *c*. Version *c* is the diary as it was published after the war. It is based on versions *a* and *b*, and is, in some places, edited by Otto Frank and the editors of the Dutch, the German and the English editions. Most readers will be familiar with version *c*. *The Diary of Anne Frank: The Revised Critical Edition* (New York: Doubleday, 2003).

What Can One Learn About Anne Frank by Reading the Novel?

The impact of the novel, *Joop ter Heul,* on the writing of Anne Frank can be seen at different levels. Comparing these may help us to understand how Anne Frank envisaged herself as a writer. Most readers of *The Diary of Anne Frank* will be familiar with the format of her diary: a series of letters to 'Kitty'. The name Kitty was derived, at least in part, from the novel *Joop ter Heul*, since, in this book, there is a character by the name of Kit Franken, who is sometimes called Kitty. The first time Anne addressed a letter to Kitty was on 22 September, 1942 in the entry that mentions *Joop ter Heul*, also for the first time. The one-line letter to 'Kitty' is the first of a series of one-line letters to all the friends of *Joop ter Heul*. In the novel, Kit is not Joop's best friend, but she is portrayed as the girl that resembles the heroine the closest. The resemblance of Kit's last name (Franken) to Anne's own name, may have added to her attractiveness for Anne. Whatever the reason, somewhere between December 1942 and December 1943, Anne decided that her diary entries would be letters to 'Kitty'.

Van Marxveldt's influence goes further than just the provision of a name, however. The form of *The Diary of Anne Frank* is modelled on the *Joop ter Heul* novel, in which the fictional Joop starts to write letters to a friend, but her father soon forbids her to correspond because he believes this interferes with her homework. Joop then turns to writing a diary, which remains the form of the rest of the novel. Anne may have compared her own prohibition to write to her friends, necessitated by the fear of being discovered, to the ban on writing to friends imposed on her fictional heroine.

In one of the most moving entries from version *a*, Anne switches from writing to a real friend to addressing fictional friends. The entry is dated 25 September, 1942, and contains a letter to Jacqueline (one of Anne's real friends) with the heading: "this is the promised fare-well letter." It is uncertain whether Anne believed that this letter would be delivered to her friend, but she wrote (or copied) it into her diary. In the letter she asks 'Jacque' to keep silent and not say anything about this letter to their friends, and Anne promises that she will explain later why this is necessary. After signing the letter, Anne turns to writing to 'Pop', the best friend of the fictional Joop. Here, Anne writes her first long letter to a fictional friend, a format she stuck to throughout the rest of the diary.

Thus, the fictional diary of *Joop ter Heul* seems to have helped Anne Frank to envisage her own writing by providing a format that allowed her to write. The direct influence of Cissy van Marxveldt can be detected in other small things. For instance, in the Netherlands during this period it was considered impolite to start letters with 'I', and, in the novel, Joop ter Heul complains about the difficulty of this rule. On 19 January, 1944, Anne writes: "Dear Kitty, I have to tell you…" and adds after 'I': "the same old mistake!" But there is another reference that is more difficult to interpret. It is found in a letter dated 22 September, 1942 in version *a*:

> …this afternoon I (…) but I had hardly sat down for a minute (to write) when I had to peel potatoes for 'her ladyship my mamma', she says it in such commanding tones, and if I don't hop to it she shouts "loos" that's German and I don't know exactly how you spell it.

This may be a reference to the fictional mother of Joop ter Heul, who is described as very demanding, or it may refer to the ignorance of the spelling of foreign languages, something that turns up regularly in the novel, where it is used to stress the fact that Joop is the youngest and least sophisticated member of her family. Either way, the references point to resemblances between the experiences of Anne Frank and those of Joop ter Heul.

There are a number of similarities between Anne Frank and the fictional Joop that are worth mentioning here. Both lived in Amsterdam, Anne living quite close to the neighbourhood of Joop ter Heul, and she may have recognised ice-cream shops and florists described in the novel – places she could herself no longer visit. Then there is Joop's strong affection for her father and her problematic relationship with her mother. Both Anne and Joop had an older sister whom they both considered more successful examples of femininity. Just like Joop, Anne had formed a club at school with her friends, and both girls tried their hand at writing poetry. One could argue that Joop's personality resembles Anne's: both are cheerful and fun-loving on the outside, but lonely, insecure and serious on the inside. These resemblances may explain, in part, why Anne liked the novel so much, and how it influenced her to the extent it did.

However, from my present-day perspective, the differences between the two girls and their texts are just as striking. In her diaries, Anne wrote about herself in relation to the larger world. She speaks about the horrors of war and anti-Semitism, and about the discrimination of women (a paragraph that has never been included in version *c*). She writes about her ambition to become a writer, and while Joop ter Heul dreams of becoming an actress, the novel is constructed in such a way that the reader cannot take this ambition seriously. Anne reflects on love and desire and about her life as a woman.

Thanks to the critical editions of her work, it is now clear that Anne Frank wrote two versions of her diary. She rewrote her first version with a view on publication after the war, hoping that it might help her to begin a career as an author. She clearly considered herself as a potential writer. When she rewrote her first version, Anne Frank carefully edited away all the references to events in the *Joop ter Huel* novels, retaining only events relating to her real life in hiding. Yet she kept Cissy van Marxvelt visible in her text. In the rewritten version, she changed her remark about Joop ter Heul from 22 September, 1942, and cited earlier, into the following sentence: "I'm thrilled with *Joop ter Heul*. I've enjoyed the whole of Cissy van Marxveldt very much. I've read *Zomerzotheid* [another novel by CvM] four times and I still laugh about some of the ludicrous situations that arise."

With this addition, Anne Frank paid tribute to the author who played such an important role in the creation of her diary. She did so in the version of her diary that she hoped would be her first publication as an author after the war. Few students/scholars can read this passage without reflecting on the irony that it was a comic novel that helped Anne Frank to create her diary, a diary that has since then been read by millions as a story with the dimensions of a tragedy.

Assignments for Student/Scholars Who Read the Novels That Have Been Read by Foremothers

➢ Collect information about the reading of your foremother during her youth. Try to find out what genres she liked, whether she had favourite novels, what access she had to reading. Did she own books, did she borrow them from friends or from a library, was her reading censored, by parents, church, or by a political system?

➤ Look for a copy of the novel that your foremother has read. Make sure you find an edition that was available to her, not a later reprint. Read the novel and collect information about the author and the book.

➤ Does the novel describe lives that resemble the life of your foremother? Include class, gender, national and ethnic identity and family relations in your analysis. Do you think that the novel confirmed a certain aspect of your foremother's life? Address gender, class, nationality and ethnicity. In what way might this confirmation have taken place? Provide arguments!

➤ Are there characters in the novel with whom your foremother may have identified consciously? In what sense could this have been the case? You can think about lived experiences, life-decisions, career-ambitions, or the position within the family. The identification may be specific and/or general.

➤ To what cultural tradition did this novel belong when your foremother read it? The novel may be part of national tradition of youth literature (lives of national heroine / hero), it may belong to 'high' or 'popular' culture, it may belong to a specific genre (novels for girls, children's books, fairy tales, educational literature, pulp fiction, romantic fiction). What does this say about the cultural location of your foremother?

➤ Compare your own reading of the novel with the way your foremother may have read it. Do you like the novel, do you identify with some of the characters, and do you recognise aspects of your own life? Do you think the novel is old-fashioned or is 'from another time'? Use the answers to these questions to reflect on resemblances and differences between your life and that of your foremother.

➤ Does the narrative of the novel resemble the life of your foremother as it is being told by her or by others? You can take this as a point of departure for reflection on the way you will structure the story of her life: you may tell a funny story, a tragic story or a heroic story.

Bibliography

http://www.annefrank.org/ The website of the Anne Frank House in Amsterdam is available in many languages and contains a wide variety of information.

Anne Frank. *The Diary of Anne Frank: The Revised Critical Edition.* New York: Doubleday, 2003.

For the shorter edition that gained world-wide fame many translations are available, see: Anne Frank, *The Diary of a Young Girl* (transl. from Dutch by B. M. Mooyaart-Doubleday with an Introduction by Eleanor Roosevelt). New York: Franklin Watts, 1952. (First English edition)

Cissy van Marxveldt. *De H.B.S. tijd van Joop ter Heul*; *Joop ter Heul serie* (School Years of Joop ter Heul; The Series Joop ter Heul). Amersfoort: Valkhoff & Co, 1934. (First published in 1919)

Cissy van Marxveldt. *Een zomerzotheid* (Midsummerfun). Amersfoort: Valkhoff & Co, 1934. (First published in 1927)

11.   *Published Diary*
Giovanna Providenti

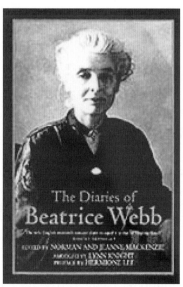

Illustration: The Diaries of Beatrice Webb book cover

Introduction

One type of source that will be encountered by students writing about foremothers is the published diary. The example that will be discussed in this paper is a page from the diary written by the sociologist and social reformer, Beatrice Potter Webb (1858–1943). Selections from these diaries have been published in two volumes, edited by Margaret I. Cole (1952).[68] The diaries, continuous, though not daily, records from 1873 to 1943, were not written for publication. However, as a source and a record they can be of immense value both for historians in general and for Women's Studies students and researchers in particular. Two editions have been published.[69] The diaries traverse a very important historical moment for social movements and for the women's movement, in which Beatrice participated. They combine

---

[68] *Beatrice Webb's Diaries* [I]: 1912-1924 / with an introduction by Lord Beveridge. [II]: 1924-1932 / with an introduction by Margaret I. Cole (Longmans, Green, 1952)

[69] After the 1952 edition, a more complete edition was published. See Norman and Jeanne MacKenzie, (eds.), *The Diary of Beatrice Webb*, (Virago, in association with The London School of Economics and Political Science, 1982-1985).

personal observations about private events with descriptions of public events.

Beatrice Potter, daughter of a wealthy industrialist, took an early interest in social problems and wrote a book about the topic entitled *Cooperative Movements in Great Britain*, published in 1891. She and her husband, Sidney Webb, played an important role in organising the British Labour Party and in founding the London School of Economics. In addition, they were of prime importance in the Fabian Society, and together wrote numerous books and articles, such as *The History of Trade Unionism* (1894; rev. ed. 1920), *Industrial Democracy* (1897), *English Local Government* (9 Vol., 1906–29), *Consumers' Cooperative Movement* (1921), and *Soviet Communism: A New Civilization?* (2 Vol., 1935), the latter written after a visit to the USSR.

On her own, Beatrice published her autobiographical *My Apprenticeship* (1926) and *Our Partnership* (1948). Her diaries were praised for their high quality: "the only English twentieth century diary to equal it is that of Virginia Woolf", wrote Robert Skidelsky in *New Society*. The diaries were edited for the first time by Margaret I. Cole who, in 1945, also wrote a biography of Beatrice Webb. The complete diaries, edited by the MacKenzies, were published between 1980 and 1985, and in 2001 an abridged version was published. The excerpt I discuss in what follows is from June 1915, the time of the First World War.

The Source

On this page of her journal, dated 22 June 1915, Beatrice Webb is speaking, in an intimate way, about an important historical moment that happened during the First World War, and what was yet not very well remembered: the International Peace Congress of Women (called the 'Hague Conference' by Webb), held at The Hague for the purpose of ending the war. The Conference was followed by the subsequent 'Peace Mission' of two delegations of women to the governments of the warring nations.

In May 1915, convened by Dr. Aletta Jacobs (Netherlands) and Jane Addams (United States), feminists gathered at The Hague, despite great obstacles, for the International Congress of Women, "to discuss what the women of the world can do and ought to do in the dreadful times in which we are now living." As Jacobs insisted in the conference call, "we feel strongly that at a time when there is so much hatred among nations, we women must show that we can retain our solidarity and that we are able to maintain a mutual friendship."[70]

The common claim from women at the Conference was to call on governments to acknowledge the necessity of involving women in political decision-making and to call for a "conference of neutral nations as an agency of continuous mediation for the settlement of the war." Besides, most of the women attending at The Hague were feminists and, as they said, "war is necessarily bound up with the destruction of feminism," and "feminism is necessarily bound up with the abolition of war."[71]

Illustration: International Congress of Women, The Hague, 1915: U.S. Delegation, see: http://www.swarthmore.edu/library/peace/Exhibits/ wilpfexhibit/1915to1919/1915to1919events.htm

[70] See Harriet Feinberg, (ed.), *Aletta Jacobs, Memories. My Life as an International Leader in Health, Suffrage and Peace*, (Trans. Annie Wright). (New York: The Feminist Press, 1996); About the Hague Women for Peace Conference and peace-feminist movement during WWI, see: Giovanna Providenti, *"Donne nonviolente in tempi di Guerra: il movimento femminista pacifista durante la prima guerra mondiale"* in *Peacekeeping non armato*, a cura di M. Pignatti Morano, "Quaderni Satyagraha", Libreria Editrice Fiorentina, 2005, 283-301; Jane Addams, Emily Green Balch and Alice Hamilton, *Women at The Hague. The International Peace Congress of 1915*, (Macmillan, 1915–New York, 2003), 98; Linda Scott, *Reconstructing Women's Thoughts. The Women's International League for Peace and for Freedom Before World War II*, (Stanford UP, 1997); Susan Zeiger, "She Didn't Raise her Boy to be a Slacker: Motherhood, Conscription, and the Culture of the First World War." *Feminist Studies*, 22, (1996), 7-40.; Barbara J. Steinson, "'The Mother Half of Humanity': American Women in the Peace and Preparedness Movements in World War I," in Carol R. Berkin and Clara. M. Lowett, (eds.), *Women, War, Revolution*, (New York: Holmes & Meier, 1980); Frances H. Early, *A World Without War: How the U.S. Feminists and Pacifists Resisted World War I*, (Syracuse UP, 1997).

[71] Quoted by Karen Offen, *European Feminisms, 1700-1950: A Political History*, (Stanford UP, 2000), 259.

Beatrice Webb, in the intimacy of a private journal, writing about the historical moment, shared deeper and more subtle information about events and about history in general. The occasion Beatrice describes is the visit of a notorious guest for dinner: Jane Addams. She was in Britain, on that day (22 June 1915), because she was going to take the St Louis transatlantic from Liverpool back to the U.S.

Jane Addams was a social reformer, pacifist and feminist who founded Hull House in Chicago in 1889 at the age of 29 and, in 1931, was awarded the Nobel Peace Prize. Her works include *Newer Ideals of Peace* (1907), *The Spirit of Youth in the City Streets* (1909), *Peace and Bread in Time of War* (1922), and her autobiographical *Twenty Years at Hull House* (1910), later followed by *The Second Twenty Years at Hull House* (1930). From the period of the First World War, Jane Addams devoted herself to the cause of peace. In 1915 she was elected as the head of the American Women's Peace Party, and was then asked to chair the Congress at The Hague. She, herself, co-authored, with Emily G. Balch and Alice Hamilton, an account of both the Congress and the Peace Mission in *Women at The Hague* (1915), recently published again (Humanity Books 2003) with an introduction by Mary Jo Deegan.

Illustration: Women's Peace Party Demonstration, ca.1915-1919.
See http://www.swarthmore.edu/library/peace/Exhibits/
wilpfexhibit/1920to1929/1920to1929.htm

On the occasion of Jane Addams' visit for dinner in the house of the Webbs, Beatrice Webb gathered interesting news from her guest about their 'missions'. Jane Addams and Beatrice Webb met in London at the 'school of socialism' in their youth and, again, in 1898 in Chicago where the Webbs were visiting the Social Settlement, Hull House (there are also some illuminating Beatrice diary pages of that occasion).[72] Furthermore, Addams quoted Beatrice Potter Webb's works in two of her books, *Newer Ideals of Peace* and *Hull-House Maps and Papers*. But what links these two women more closely is that they had the same political agenda: working for democracy, justice and peace.

The following source is a draft from *Beatrice Webb's Diaries*.[73]
Year 1915

June 22nd. Jane Addams, with whom we stayed at Hull House, Chicago, on our first world tour, dined with us last night. Since we met her seventeen years ago, she has become a world celebrity – the most famous woman of the U.S.A. representing the best aspects of the Feminist Movement and the most distinguished elements in the social reform movement. Some say that she has been too much in the limelight lately and that she is no longer either as sane or as subtle in her public utterances. But to us she seemed the same gentle, dignified, sympathetic woman, though like the rest of us she has lost in brilliancy and personal charm – the inevitable result of age, fame and being overtly occupied. Her late mission to the governments of the world, as the leading representative of neutral women at the Hague Conference, has brought her into still greater prominence. She and one or two other women from the neutral countries were in charge of the "Peace Mission" to the Governments of Germany, Austria, Hungary, Italy, France, Belgium and England. She had found Sir Edward Grey politely encouraging, expressing his own

[72] About this visit, see Robyn Muncy, *Creating a Female Dominion in American Reform, 1890-1935*, (Oxford UP, 1991); Allen F. Davis and Mary Lynn McCree, (eds.), *Eighty Years at Hull-House* (Chicago: Quadrangle, 1969), 66.

[73] Margaret I. Cole (ed.), *Beatrice Webb's Diaries*, (Longmans, Green, 1952), 40-41.

personal pacific sentiments, but saying nothing about his government.

The French Ministers were decidedly hostile - the most hostile of all the governments – to any "Peace manoeuvres"; the Italians were boys with a new toy; the Hungarians were deliberately oncoming; they showed no hatred of England or Russia; disclaiming all responsibility for the treatment of Belgium, "that is Germany's affair", and suggesting that it might be quite easy for them to make peace with Russia separately. As for the rest of the war, it did not concern them. The Hungarian government even permitted a public meeting at which the women delegates pleaded for peace. The Austrians, on the other hand, were nervous and depressed but pretended complete confidence and refused to commit themselves. Jane Addams was most interesting in her description of Berlin. To outward seeming everything was prosperous and easy, the whole population united and confident. But there was a grimness, a restrained misery that manifested itself in bitterness against England and the U.S.A. They had thrashed Russia and if they chose to sacrifice the men they could break through in France: Italy was negligible. In spite of this appearance of brutal self-confidence the Chancellor and Foreign Secretary was far more willing to listen to peace proposals and even to encourage her to promote peace than any of the other Governments. Bethmann-Hollweg [Chancellor of Germany in 1909, dismissed in 1917 [M. I. C.] was terribly distressed at the loss of life: he had lost his son: every family was in mourning; they could win, but at what a cost! The longer the war lasted the more difficult it would be to persuade the military party to give up Belgium: the sooner peace came, the more reasonable Germany could afford to be. Though Jane Addams did not suggest it herself, I should gather that Germany feels to be at the top of her fortunes and would be glad to entertain proposals before another winter in the trenches. Bethmann-Hollweg even suggested that there might be a conference of neutral powers with representatives of the belligerents. They would not accept the U.S.A. as arbiter and looked to Sweden or Spain as the initiator of peace. In the eyes of the American public no one in Berlin seemed in the least concerned about the effect, of the sinking of the Lusitania. "The Americans cannot fight," remarked Sudicum [Dr. Südekum was a German Social-Democrat of the Right, a friend of Noske and Walter Rathenau, and member from 1914 onwards of the *Mittwochs-Gesellschaft*, an all-party luncheon club M. I. C.] contemptuously, "their opinion of our doings is really of no account."

Jane Addams herself thinks it inconceivable that the U.S.A. should come into the war, and she clearly sees little or no difference between British and German policy, either before or during the war – at least that is the impression she leaves. Her message to us was "the neutrality of the seas."[74]

Learning from the Source
This type of historical source will provide students with three important issues about the politics of memory.

Public History and Private Memories
The diary fragment describes several historical events that have also been described by historians in books mentioned in this text. Students can be invited to compare historical studies about the First World War, about the history of women's peace movements, about connections and tensions between British and American women's movements during the period in question, and about Webb's attitude to her own government regarding the war with Germany. This will shed light on the way history books differ from contemporary private sources. Students may also reflect on the way Webb's private journal differs from her own political statements at this time. They may try to

---

[74] This page is taken from M. I. Cole, (ed.), *Beatrice Webb's Diaries*, (1952), 40-41. However, there exists a newer and extended edition: Norman MacKenzie and Jeanne MacKenzie, (eds.), *The Diaries of Beatrice Webb*, (abridged by Lynn Knight, preface by Hermione Lee), (Northeastern UP), 630.

find public statements made by Beatrice Webb about the war, and compare these with the tone and contents of her diary.

Diaries Between Public and Private Texts

Beatrice Webb published two books about her life. The diaries were only published after her death. Reviewers have remarked how the publication of the diaries offers readers a more complete, less complimentary, but definitely more interesting, image of Beatrice Webb. Students may compare the diaries to the published autobiographical books and see what they can learn about self-fashioning. Students may also think about the issue of imagined readers of this (and any) diary. Did Webb write her journal only for her own eyes, or did she use the notes about political visits in her political activism? Did she have in mind the possibility of publication of parts of her diary later?

Public and Private Sphere

A third issue that this diary opens up is the way private and public spheres mingle in politics. One can ask about the way British politics are conducted in the decades around 1900. Political history is often cast in public narratives, but diaries like this indicate the importance of private meetings as encounters where political strategies are discussed and deals are made. In the eighteenth century, women played a part in political history through their role as hostesses of *salons;* in the course of the nineteenth century a more formalised public sphere was developed for politics in which parliaments, journals, and political parties were organised. Women were mostly excluded from these forms of public agency, their role being defined as belonging to the domestic sphere. Domesticity and, therefore, women, carried connotations of love, peace and care.

The women's movement claimed a public role for women. The Hague Conference is an example of this strategy: feminists used the format of an international conference, and an international mission, to advocate their ideas. On the other hand, many feminists used the domestic values as an argument why women should enter public life.[75] Women advocating peace fitted the image of womanhood. Using a dinner party, such the one organised by Beatrice Webb as an example, one could discuss the ambiguous relationship of feminists to this distinction between public and private spheres.

Assignment
> ➢ Look for descriptions of the women's peace conference in history books about the First World War. Compare your findings with the diary. Did Beatrice Webb take a public stance in this?
> ➢ Compare the page cited from Webb's diary with her published autobiography. Describe how the two texts differ, and discuss the 'imagined reader' of both texts.
> ➢ Compare Karen Offen's description (see *European Feminisms*) of the Hague Conference and the peace mission with the diary-entry. In what sense do these texts differ? What can you learn from these different types of text?[76]
> ➢ Would you describe the dinner party with Jane Addams as a private or public event? Provide arguments!
> ➢ How would you describe the opinion of Beatrice Webb about Jane Addams? Look for signs of ambivalence in the text, and compare your findings with other descriptions of personal relations in the women's movement.[77]

---

[75] See Ellen Dubois, Mari Jo Buhle, Temma Kaplan, Gerda Lerner, Carroll Smith-Rosenberg, "Politics and Culture in Women's History: A Symposium." *Feminist Studies*, Vol. 6 (1980), afl.1, 26.

[76] Karen Offen, *European Feminisms, A Political History 1700-1950*, (Stanford UP, 2000).

[77] Mineke Bosch, *Politics and Friendship: Letters from the International Woman Suffrage Alliance, 1902-1942*, (Ohio State UP, 1990).

12. Autobiography
Ritva Nätkin

Illustration: Cover of book by Ritva Nätkin.

Introduction

When I was a child, my mother used to tell me that, in war-time, she had heard it constantly repeated on radio broadcasts that 'there are too few of us' and 'that is why we will lose the war'. My mother taught me that, ironically, having a lot of children was a kind of national service on the home-front. Because my father had been wounded in the Winter War against the Soviet Union (1939), and had never returned to the front, conceiving and bearing children was a kind of compensatory act. I was born as the sixth and last of a town-dwelling family's children. My mother's patriotic story was not straightforward because it also included contradictions, poverty and sickness at the time I was born, and, of course, detailed descriptions of childbirth, my mother's bravery and joy about the babies. However, my mother's story included a message of feminine ingenuity in overcoming the obstacles, which, on a more general level, seems to have been the reason for narrating the life stories of those I have analysed.

I have read and interpreted the autobiographies of Finnish women written in 1991, which talked about mothering in the decades from the 1940s to the 1980s. These autobiographies are unpublished stories, gathered for research purposes, and stored in the Folklore Archive of the Finnish Literature Society; the collection is named *Satasärmäinen nainen* ('Women with a hundred angles and wheels'). It was for my dissertation that I chose 50 stories out of 651 in order to separate 'a story of mothering' from them.[78] My research question asked how Finnish mothers answered the invitation to be national agents, and how they responded to the nationalist discourses in their narratives of motherhood, through analysing the conventions and plot structures used in their narration. Was the motive of the authors to have a child as patriotic as my own mother had been? Did women sacrifice themselves to the family, motherhood and the nation also in autobiographies? My mother heard the call of the nationalist discourse, and it is evident in the autobiographies that other women did too.

The Genre of Autobiographies

Anni Vilkko has written about the narrative analysis of women's autobiographies.[79] She states that autobiography is "a serious genre" where the authors pay much attention to construct it in order to achieve completeness. She also says, quoting Nancy K. Miller, that the writer makes a so-called autobiographical contract when she reads the contest announcement and answers it. There are different ways to read an autobiography: it can be interpreted as an (literary) entity, or cut into parts or themes.

---

[78] I wrote my dissertation entitled *Kamppailu suomalaisesta äitiydestä. Maternalismi, väestöpolitiikka ja naisten kertomukset*, (Struggle for Finnish Motherhood, Maternalism, Population Policy and Women's Narratives), (Helsinki: Gaudeamus, 1997) at the University of Tampere.

[79] See Helmi Järviluoma, Pirkko Moisala and Anni Vilkko (eds.), *Gender and Qualitative Methods*, (London: SAGE, 2003), 46-68.

The story of motherhood I interpreted is part of the women's autobiographies. In the case of most of the writers, this takes up, on average, about a third of the autobiography's pages. Motherhood is situated in-between childhood or youth and old age, and it seems inevitable to involve the man with whom the woman conceived the children. Some writers have dedicated their whole story to this stage: pregnancies, births, child-care and sexual relations, but, for most, motherhood is a separate stage of life. Only the beginning of the story is clearly distinguishable, and this is seldom the case at the end. In most stories on motherhood, I had a difficult time counting the exact number of pages, as I had to decide in each case to what extent the relationship with the man (or several men), grandchildren, or the general construction of family life (such as building a house, for example), were part of the story of motherhood. The difficulties in discerning the end of this part of the story has, in my mind, to do with the fact that untangling oneself from motherhood usually happens gradually, and the intensity of mothering decreases as the children grow older. There were big differences among the narrators, for example, in whether they had things to say about their lives after the motherhood stage.

There is also reason to ask what the writers wanted to communicate when they submitted their writings into the *Satasärmäinen nainen* contest in 1991, or how the writers came to be selected in the first place.[80] The contest was organised by The Kalevala[81] Women's Association, which was founded by Finnish women's associations. Thus, on a very general level, it can be assumed that the writers wanted to make comments on 'Finnishness'. On the other hand, the organisers may not have had such as big an influence as the name of the contest itself, which was a guideline to the writers. According to the invitation, the woman had permission to write about their 'hundred edges', in other words, in diverse ways about their lives and, also, about the controversies included in their lives. The contest flyer encouraged women to use their own styles to write "frankly and openly" about what it is like to be a Finnish woman. In order to make things clear it was said that the writers could also write

[80] About the contest, see, Ulla Piela ed., *Aikanaisia*, (Helsinki: Finnish Literature Society, 1993).
[81] Finnish national epos.

about their families, their jobs and hobbies, and crisis situations, happy moments and dreams.

The women wrote surprisingly often about the subordination they had encountered from their relatives, families and men in general. Among my data there was a lot of talk about single motherhood and difficult relationships with men. Some researchers seem to think that the writings did not describe 'Finnishness' well enough. For example, Satu Apo claims, in her own article in the researcher anthology,[82] that, in the autobiographical data of *Satasärmäinen nainen*, the women describe the relationships in the society in the countryside in such a contentious way that she thinks those autobiographies cannot necessarily be regarded as representations of Finnish life: "I think that especially sensitive and in one way or another 'chipped' people have wanted to tell their stories". She has read some of the same stories as I have, yet I did not have doubts about the authenticity or representativeness of the material; I was not expecting a more romanticised or harmonious description of Finnish life.

Kirsti Määttänen, in her article in the same anthology,[83] gives a more satisfactory answer to the problem of how the writers came to be selected. In my opinion, she also answers the question as to why, in my own data, the stories written by single mothers seem to be the most patriotic: "By telling their stories the writers create a sense of unity and continuity for themselves and about themselves. If their lives have included hard experiences and fates, people may have a stronger need to make sense of them than otherwise would be the case. On the other hand, the most difficult fates will always remain outside autobiographical collections."

The National Context

Finnish women are said to be hard-working, and the male breadwinner model in Finland is considered weak. This can be partly explained by the wars fought on Finnish soil – the Civil War in 1918 and the wars against the Soviet Union in 1939 and 1941-45 – as well as the heavy casualties and sparse population. According to the population propaganda at the time of the last war and its aftermath,

---

[82] Piela, (ed.), 1993, 127.
[83] *ibid.*, 162.

there were 'too few of us'; the country had to be both reconstructed and repopulated. It was expected that every family should produce 4-6 children, so that the Finnish population would not decrease. The 'baby boom' generations were born at the end of the 1940s, a time when the nationalistic emphasis on the united population who survived was strong, and this can be regarded as the life-force of the welfare state which developed later. The population policy also includes a strong idealisation of motherhood and a glorification of the value of motherhood. The mother is the crucial person when decisions about the growth of populations are made. Along with population policy, the welfare and well-being of mothers became national property. Nira Yuval-Davis writes that one of the most essential tasks of women in nationalist projects is to act as biological reproducers and generators of new populations.[84]

Population policy also concentrates on women's bodies in the role of giving birth, even to the extent that one can talk about nationalising the female body. The scientific discoveries and procedures that have to do with giving birth and child-care, and the propaganda and education that they entailed were so compelling that it can be said that an ordinary woman – a mother – was conceived as the metaphoric soil for nationalistic aims in the population policy. I think that, in Finland, this soil was over-exploited and its nourishment was neglected because the mothers were left on their own to burn out with their large families and double duty of paid work and child-care.

The most contradictory issue after the war was by far illegal abortion, with professionals regarding the situation among the citizens as explosive. Many more abortions were performed than is the case today. After the war, the estimate is 30,000 per year, and most of these were illegal. The Population and Welfare Federation, delegated by the National Board of Health, issued statements on abortion, where it interpreted the first 1950 law on abortion, but granted abortion usually only on medical grounds, or denied it altogether. In the texts that I have analysed, the Federation's 'work against abortion' is very prominent, and abortion was regarded almost as an unpatriotic act. There were huge regional differences within the country. There were large families (10-15 children per family) in the North and East of

---

[84] Nira Yuval Davis, *Gender and Nation*, (London: Sage Publications, 1997).

Finland, often in religious communities. Smaller families (with two children) and more modern attitudes were found in the southern part of the country, evident, for example, in attitudes to abortion, contraception and contraceptives. The Finns were in a very unequal position as regards abortion and the availability of contraceptives. The poor families with many children in the countryside were characterised by the word 'raggedy'.

Abortions were a direct threat to population growth. The mother's health in the future was also at stake because the quackery involved in illegal abortions caused "fevered miscarriages" and permanent infertility.[85] Many children were born in very risky social conditions and there was much social distress. The problem of abortion and its solutions had a number of competing constructs: it was debated whether medical, eugenic, criminal or social indications were grounds for granting abortion.

Abortion being regarded as unpatriotic related to its association with socialism and the Soviet Union (the former and present Russia). The abortion controversy was solved by the relatively liberal Abortion Act in 1971. Counselling on contraception started at that time and protection of motherhood was improved, while both of these aspects were enacted in the Public Health Act in 1972. Legislation enabling forced sterilisation was repealed.

When I diligently looked for mentions of abortions (legal or illegal) in my data, which I knew had happened relatively frequently at the time, I found very few examples. As abortion was forbidden, in fact a criminalised and shameful experience from the 1940s to well into the 1960s, it was not talked about in the autobiographical texts. Women would also have found it difficult to write about failed motherhood, such as abandoning one's own children. The authors, thus, seem to be products of their own era in a way that, even if they wrote their stories in the early 1990s, they used the concepts and

---

[85] In my dissertation (Nätkin 1997, 127-133) I also analysed the discussions of professionals. In the Population and Welfare Federation's clinics (called 'marriage centres' or 'social problem centres'), the doctors tried to obligate mothers seeking abortion to carry the pregnancies to term because the society, with its family policy benefits, had 'done so much'. Women were bluntly made liable. Doctors persuaded the mothers seeking abortion to give birth to 'one more baby' before they were granted permission to contraception or sterilisation. Doctors also gave medical interpretations for the women's wish to terminate their pregnancies as first trimester depression, which could be treated and cured.

narrative conventions of the time to describe the feelings of the period. My data, evidently, also turned out to be a part of the national project.

The women did not mention illegal abortions at all and they wrote very little about abortion in general. They would write, rather, about what it was like at the clinic to try to keep alive a woman who had tried to self-abort, or what it felt like to see foetuses wrapped up in black cloth in the dustbins of the hospital when what you yourself suffered from was childlessness, or what it felt like to hear one's own mother talk about how she had planned an abortion. A few descriptions in the data were about abortion in the third person: the writer says that 'she' had an abortion, but says at the same time that 'she' is largely herself. Some say that the clear and authoritarian denial of abortion from the doctor had made it easier for them to make the decision, as they had prevaricated. One woman even wrote that "she was offered an abortion but she refused".

Abortion or No Abortion?

One writer in the data – I will call her Selma – went into a lot of details when she described the thoughts she had had about having an abortion. She has given birth to six children but, from time to time, rebelled and threatened to stop having children after number three. Selma brought up these thoughts at the end of her narrative when she had already written about everything else: "I had three children already and I was about to give up the fourth. Then I started to think differently. This child was connected to me with its umbilical cord; it had its own heart, and eyebrows like little paintbrushes. It was so tiny but I started to eat yeast and mortar, didn't I have impossible cures? When the child was born it was over four kilos but I was like a ghost."

In the 1940s and '50s, having an abortion, terminating a pregnancy, would not have fitted in with the spirit of the times. Because of the mother's exhaustion, a pregnancy could be terminated, but clear medical indication was needed. Selma chose a different path and gave birth to three more children. Several other women with a large number of children have stories where the narrative, in a way, stops after 2-3 children, and where they would like to use birth control, although they later have a few more children. Selma says that her decision was influenced by the fact that she defined the foetus as a baby by imagining what it looked like in the womb. Ironically, the child, whose pregnancy the mother had planned to terminate, later ended up having an operation and being seriously ill. Selma felt as if life had revenged the thoughts about abortion in a grotesque way: "When the operating day came they shaved the child bald. Wearing a kerchief on its head it looked just like a Bedouin. 'You won't cry, mother, if I die?' the child asked and I said firmly that I wouldn't although I could already feel the tears behind the bones in my forehead. Several hours later on that same day the doctor came to say: 'The surgeon's knife has done what it can; now it is the turn of the mother's love and God's miracle'."

Selma chose to have six children – a decision that went well with the population policy – with professional support. She felt that the doctor had taken her on board a team consisting of the holy trinity of God, the surgeon's knife and, now, the mother's love.[86] When the seventh pregnancy was terminated, Selma wrote that "the milk was flowing, but there wasn't anybody to feed". It was like her body was demanding more babies, but she herself couldn't bear any more.

It is worth noting that this patriotic spirit and responsible attitude is most often mentioned by single mothers. The above writer, Selma, was a single parent for some time after she had encountered violence from her husband. Another writer, a much younger one, Liisa, was the single parent of five children when she wrote her story. Liisa, who gave birth to her children in the 1970s and '80s, writes about when her contraception, the coil, failed, and the doctor had offered an abortion. She was in an insecure economic position as the single parent of four children and the father did not want the child. But Liisa did. The figure of the doctor helped her outlive the controversial situation:

> Every day when the anxiety started to get insufferable I heard the consoling voice of my conscience; or maybe it was my gynaecologist's voice: 'You are the mother type. I appreciate your kind of women. You will be fine.' These words can be thought of as my own thoughts because I also describe myself with such

---

[86] According to the discussions of professionals, which I read for my analysis, midwives belonged to the teams and they took great responsibility for a new life. This team was called 'God's colleagues' in the Midwives' trade document.

words. Because, if I want to be honest, no women would make it with this burden, without an explanation.

When Liisa says that the doctor was her conscience, she describes the way in which she constructed herself as a member of the society. Her relationship with her doctor reveals her capacities as a citizen where motherhood had a significant role. According to Liisa, it was valuable – in fact, the measure of womanhood – to survive alone with the heavy burden. It can be seen that during the war and in its aftermath, women were invited as national actors into the same teams with professionals, and it was especially the single mothers whose writing suggests that they accepted this invitation.

Why Was Women's Agency Needed?
After the Second World War, Finland favoured population growth and the unity of the nation, for which the agency of women was needed and valued. The mother is the crucial person when decisions about population increases are made. Along with population policy, the mother's welfare and well-being became national property. The population policy was one of the (strongest) discourses in civil society during the war and its aftermath. Also, women's associations, which were promoting 'maternalist' women's politics and feminism, were active in doing this.[87]

Finnish women also needed to be strong at that time. In Finland, where the male breadwinner model was weak, women had to construct their family's lives on their own irreplaceable position. This emphasis also reflects submission to the fact that they had no other choice. The Finnish legend – the war widow or some other woman solely responsible for many children – lives on in these stories. It is also a narrative strategy, the function of which is to defend and reassure oneself against the fact that the single parent could be suspected of bad mothering or being immoral, as was the case a couple of decades ago. In a way, the woman who experienced single motherhood struggled over her place in the category of (good) mothers and simultaneously (over)emphasised its aspects.

---

[87] Ritva Nätkin, "Women's Agency in Finnish Population Policy 1941-1971: A Maternalist Policy." *Österreichische Zeitschrift für Geschichtswissenschaften, (Austrian Journal for Historical Studies)*, 15:1 (2004), 75-92.

Interviews

13.   *Interview*
Patricia Chiantera-Stutte

Illustration: Luce Fabbri (courtesy of Paolo Finzi and the editors of A)

The Context

The source chosen is an interview with Luce Fabbri, a feminist and anarchist, which appeared in the anarchist review *A*, Issue 247 No. 28. (Summer 1998). *A* is a very influential Italian review on anarchism, well-read not only in Italy, but also world-wide. It deals with several themes, from the most important historical anarchists, to the history of anarchism; from contemporary political issues to social and economic problems.

The interview with Luce Fabbri took place in Italy and it was led by Cristina Valenti. Fabbri is an important exponent of anarchism: she was the daughter of well-known Italian Anarchist Luigi Fabbri, friend and collaborator of Errico Malatesta. She continued the political and cultural activity promoted by her father, who founded the review *Studi sociali*. The Interview deals with Luce Fabbri's life experiences, with her memories of the flight of her family from Italy and fascism to Uruguay, with memories of her father and of other anarchist thinkers, and with her conception of anarchism.

Luce Fabbri is a very important figure in the anarchist movement: her theory of anarchism derives from both liberalism and socialism. For her, the only way to build a society based on justice and respect for the individual is in the development of solidarity and human freedom. Her theory takes its origin from the experience and rejection of all forms of totalitarianism, including fascism, Nazism and communism. For this reason, Fabbri's work is more and more widely discussed and read nowadays in many countries: she was one of the few intellectuals who pointed out, without fear, the consequences of Russian communism during the Cold War, while at the same time criticising the American model of capitalism.

Interview Summary

The interview begins with some questions on the social and familial *milieu* of Luce Fabbri. In response to the question on the origins of her anarchism, Fabbri replies that two factors were significant: her family and the experience of the First World War. She says: "I am the daughter of an Anarchist and I was educated with libertarian criteria. I breathed the liberty in the family, liberty on our [anarchist] terms."[88] About her memory of the First World War she explains that:

> what influenced and constituted my point of departure for anarchism was the First World War. I was deeply impressed by it, because we had a lot of friends in the war, and they came along as they left for the war. Bernieri[89] [Italian anarchist] came along when he was recalled for military service, some fugitives came along after Caporetto,[90] some deserters came to see us. I felt the war atmosphere ... the tales that I heard impressed me, but above all I was indignant with the fact that there was power, which was capable of obliging a person not only of being killed, but also of killing someone ... It was inconceivable for me that there could be

---

[88] *"Sono figlia di un anarchico e sono stata educata con criteri libertari. Respiravo la libertà in famiglia, la libertà in senso nostro".*

[89] Bernieri was a very influential Italian anarchist.

[90] Caporetto was the name of a battlefield, which determined the defeat of the Italian army during the First World War.

someone who could say to another 'kill a person who did not do anything to you. Otherwise I will kill you'.[91]

Besides her father, Luce Fabbri also remembers her mother to be a very important figure in her life. Luce's mother was not an anarchist, but her influence was strong, as was her support. To the question of whether her family model was her father rather than her mother, Fabbri answers: "no, it was both of them! Both were libertarian. What my mother did not like was the violence. She did not agree that the insurrection was the way to build a free society. However, for the rest I think she would have been with us".[92]

The second part of the interview is about Fabbri's migration from fascist Italy to Uruguay, and about the anarchist movement during and after the Second World War. In particular, Fabbri shows her analysis of the failures of the anarchist movement during the war in Spain. Regarding the seizure of power by anarchists in Spain, Fabbri expresses her doubts and her criticisms. As the anarchists seized the government, it was an absolutely incoherent act, but many, many lives of militants were in danger ... probably it was necessary to leave a way open, in order to save them.[93] However, about the transformation of the voluntary anarchic force into a military force, Fabbri declares: "this was an even bigger mistake, because it had very serious consequences. It compromised not only the revolution but also the war. Her opposition to violence and the war are expressed in the last part of the interview when she speaks about her activity as a teacher and her idea of anarchism. Teaching must remain a libertarian

---

[91] *"Quello che ha influito moltissimo e che penso sia stato il vero punto di partenza del mio anarchismo fu la prima guerra mondiale. M'ha veramente impressionato, in modo profondo, perché avevamo molti amici al fronte e tanti di loro passavano da noi quando partivano, è passato Berneri quando è stato richiamato, sono passati alcuni fuggiaschi dopo Caporetto, venivano a trovarci i disertori. L'atmosfera della guerra l'ho sentita molto ... I racconti che ascoltavo m'impressionavano molto ma soprattutto mi indignava il fatto che ci fosse un potere capace di obbligare una persona non solo a farsi ammazzare, ma ad ammazzare. Mi sembrava inconcepibile che ci fosse qualcuno che potesse dire ad un altro "ammazza uno che non ti ha mai fatto niente altrimenti ti fucilo."*

[92] *No, tutti e due! Perché libertari lo erano entrambi: l'educazione era la stessa. Quello che a mia madre non piaceva era la violenza, non era molto convinta che l'insurrezione fosse il mezzo più normale per arrivare ad una società libera. Ma per il resto credo che probabilmente sarebbe stata insieme a noi.*

[93] *Quando gli anarchici sono andati al governo, fu senz'altro un atto di assoluta incoerenza, però era in pericolo la vita di migliaia, migliaia e migliaia di militanti ... Forse fu necessario lasciare una strada aperta perché potessero salvarsi.*

practice for Fabbri, who tried to free the school from the political influences of reactionary and communist parties.

According to Fabbri, the most important value in anarchism is represented by the liberty of each person and by solidarity in the economic field. Her anarchism is "libertarian socialism". She says:

> Liberty and socialism have not to be considered opposite elements ... but ones that are strictly inherent in each other. What distinguishes us from the social democrats, for example, is that they think that it is possible to conciliate socialism with liberty through compromises, while we think that socialism is liberty and that we cannot create it without liberty. And liberty must be based on solidarity, because without solidarity we cannot achieve liberty.[94]

Fabbri's main idea is the refusal of violence. She believes that:

> in order to gain liberty we need peace, not only peace between social groups but an interior peace, a growing reciprocal tolerance. If the anarchist movement does not have this function, i.e. one of giving an example of pacific coexistence among all differences, a dialectical, polemic and nevertheless pacific coexistence, what other kind of function would it have?[95]

Analysis
This interview allows us to see how Luce Fabbri perceived herself, her family, her political *milieu* and all political events from her childhood, and also how she developed her own political activity. On the one hand, it is interesting to see how she perceives the position of her

---

[94] *"La libertà e il socialismo non vanno considerati come elementi opposti ... ma come strettamente inerenti l'uno all'altro. Quello che ci distingue dai socialdemocratici, per esempio, è che loro pensano che si debba conciliare il socialismo con la libertà attraverso delle forme di compromesso mentre noi riteniamo che il socialismo è libertà e che non lo si può costruire senza libertà. E la libertà dev'essere basata sulla solidarietà perché senza solidarietà non è realizzabile. Dunque libertà e socialismo non vanno intesi come valori contrari che hanno bisogno di essere conciliati, come molti hanno voluto sostenere."*

[95] *"per arrivare alla libertà ci voglia la pace, non solo la pace tra i gruppi sociali, ma anche una pace interiore, una maggior tolleranza reciproca. Se il movimento anarchico non assolve a questa funzione, quella di fornire un esempio di convivenza pacifica fra tutte le differenze, una convivenza dialettica e polemica però pacifica, che altra funzione può disimpegnare?"*

mother as an important figure, not politically active, but important in order to support the private life of her family. On the other hand, it is striking to see the role of Luce Fabbri in juxtaposition to her mother, as a woman visible in the public sphere and who took on the role of her father in the anarchistic struggles.

Moreover, Fabbri is a person whose life has been conditioned by violence and war: her decision to be an anarchist was also due to her experience of war. In this respect, we can analyse her as a public and politically active figure, who not only suffered the violence of the war, but who struggled against it. Apparently the figure of her father and of the anarchistic *milieu* was a precondition of her consciousness. Therefore, she remembers, with particular affection, one of her father's friends, Errico Malatesta. The link between her generation and the generation of her parents is very solid, as can be sensed from what she says about her ideal of autonomy, and what she also teaches to her students, stimulated by her father, who told her: 'you must think with your head'.

Assignment

The students are asked to think about their relation to the figure of Luce Fabbri and to relate her to their personal experience and to their familiar *milieu*.

> ➤ How do you feel about the figure of Luce Fabbri?
> ➤ Do you think she is related to an old generation? Has she got something to say to you?
> ➤ Do you think that her struggle is utopian and has nothing to do with reality?
> ➤ Compare her figure to the figure of your female 'role model'.
> ➤ Compare her figure to the figure of your mother and grandmother: are they totally different? Do they have something in common?
> ➤ Do you think that Luce Fabbri is an 'exception', or do you think that many women reacted to the war by refusing violence? Do you know any of them? Can you tell their story? Can you interview them?

14. *Interviews with Women Who Work in a Profession that is Considered Masculine*
Martine Jaminon

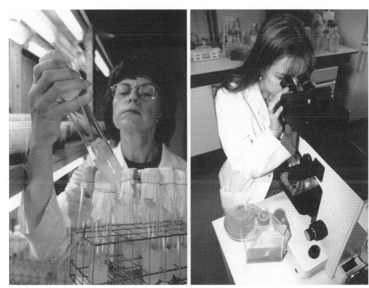

Illustrations: Women in Science.
(http://www.presse.ulg.ac.be/photos/recherche.html)

Background

The European labour market is heavily gendered. This is the case for skilled and unskilled labour as well as for professions. Many professions (Law, Medicine, Science, Theology) came into existence as exclusively male fields. The late-nineteenth and twentieth centuries witnessed the struggle of women to enter these fields with more or less success. In many countries 'the first woman medical doctor', 'the first woman who practised law' are remembered. Their names are sometimes used for institutions, prizes or organisations that support women in certain professions. Today, women are still exceptional or in small minorities in many professions. For female students being trained for a professional career, it is important to reflect on the impact of this gendering on their own life plan. This short article will describe how a teacher can invite students who are considering a professional career in a male-defined profession, to think about gender issues.

The source material that could be used for this assignment includes interviews or short biographies of women who have made their livelihood in science, a professional field that is dominated by men. The disparity of women-men or girls-boys in scientific jobs or studies has been dealt with only very recently – for most of the twentieth century, science was a field of studies chosen by men, and women scientists are mainly famous because they are so very rare.[96]

It is a great challenge to overcome the numerous difficulties associated with getting more girls and women interested in science. If Europe wants to assure its future economic life, then it has to invest, today, in education in the field of sciences and technologies. This is the only way to maintain the critical, required number of high-level scientists and technicians. Since the middle of the 1990s, various public reports, published in industrialised countries, display an alarming lack of such highly qualified women. The situation may get worse still, since young people seem to be less and less interested in science. It is clear, then, that a larger involvement of women in science is not only a key factor to increase the critical mass of scientists, but, also, an urgently required addition to the excellence of science as a whole. However, it seems obvious that the majority of young women are still not inclined to choose scientific or technical studies, which would lead them to a professional career, usually seen as traditionally reserved for men.[97]

By offering students life stories of women in science, and by inviting them to read and interrogate such stories, students may find a way to identify with these women, and to reconsider their own preferences and prejudices about women in science. The source material can be used in very different contexts: primary and secondary schools, teacher-training colleges, students in scientific curricula as

---

[96] Marie Curie is the obvious example. See Evelyn Fox Keller, *A Feeling for the Organism: The Life and Work of Barbara McClintock,* (San Francisco: W.H. Freeman, 1983).

[97] See, for example, S. Clegg, "Theorising the Machine: Gender, Education and Computing." *Gender and Education* 13, (2001), 307-324; B. Elkjaer, "Myth and Reality About Women and Technology," in *Proceedings of the IFIP TC 9/WG 9.1 International Conference on Women, Work and Computerization,* (Amsterdam: NHPC, 1989); Rogers and J. Duffield, "Factors Underlying Persistent Gendered Option Choices in School Science and Technology in Scotland," *Gender and Education,* 12.3, (2000), 367-383; E. Spertus, "Why Are There so Few Female Computer Scientists?" *AI lab Technical Report* 1315, (1991).

future teachers or future firm managers: masters programmes in sciences, anthropology, sociology or 'history of sciences' programmes.

The pedagogical and political objectives of such an assignment may be diverse: it will make young girls and boys aware of the problem, it may encourage girls in starting a scientific career and it may offer ways to establish links between scientific politics and real work conditions. The assignment can make boys and girls aware of problems that women encounter in their professional life, and to modify their way of seeing and doing when they hold, or will try to hold, high level positions. The following is a list of suggestions that can be adjusted depending on the level of the classroom and on its main fields of interest. They have not been tested yet. However, they are presented in the framework of a continued training for teachers in secondary school. An e-learning platform will be devoted to this problem where teachers will be allowed to exchange information about their practice of the suggested lectures.

Example of an Interview

Anne-Marie TRULLEMANS
Professor at the Faculty of Applied Sciences
Louvain Catholic University,
DICE (Electronic Circuits and Devices, Electricity Department)

> Can you tell us more about your career path before you became a teacher here?

> *I studied engineering. I was the only girl at the time. The previous girl had just graduated. She had been the only female student for five years, as was the case with me! After that, I worked as an assistant and prepared my PhD at the same time. I was working on the MOS transistor, that had just been discovered, and on the bipolar transistor. After my thesis I worked for some time in the same microelectronics lab, before moving to the telecom department where my expertise seemed useful. Later I came back here, in microelectronics, to develop circuit simulation programmes, and I was granted a position as*

'premier assistant', meaning a tenured position. I gave supply classes from time to time, which is how I took part in several courses in the microelectronics section. Amongst others, I give a course on computer aided design and on the methodology of digital circuits and also one on electronics for future business engineers, at ICHEC. And in the context of first-year studies in engineering I am involved in a project designed to help students master basic notions in electricity.

Besides teaching, is research still an important aspect of your activities?

Yes, it is. What I particularly appreciate in research is discovering and exploring a subject. I also like being in touch with other scientists. With modern communication media, it is absolutely incredible; we are no longer confined to our laboratories. Researchers from all over the world have come to work in our lab, and we can keep in touch with all of them. International collaborations also allow us to travel. And we have many contacts with people from the industry as well.

You said you were the only girl in your promotion. Why did you make this rather uncommon choice?

I think I had always been interested in everything scientific. I do not think my family had influenced me, because even if my father was an engineer, he did not push me into this direction. He rather imagined me working in the actuary field or something of the kind, to have a job in a Ministry, which he thought was very good. I wanted to move and discover the world. Science in action interested me, rather than science in theory. And I wanted to make something useful for society. I could have studied medicine, because I liked life sciences very much, but I was not very fond of chemistry and memorising was a problem for me. I preferred understanding rather than remembering. So, I realised that engineer studies would suit me. I gathered information, saw it was possible – or at least, not forbidden. I enrolled thinking "I will try" and, since everything I tried worked, I continued. And I am not at all unhappy with my choice! It really corresponds to what I wanted to do.

Did your high school teachers approve of your choice?

My math teacher entirely supported me. She was a nun, very short, really open and dynamic, with a remarkably inquisitive mind. But, as everyone at the time, I had had to take orientation tests in high school, and someone had found that scientific studies did not suit me. I never understood how they came to that conclusion. It is true that I did not really like those tests, and only grudgingly took them!

You have two children, was it difficult to manage both your career and your family life?

I cannot really say I have had real difficulties. I've always worked full-time… It is a question of organisation. You have to decide what you can and cannot do: it is not necessarily easy to travel a lot and leave your home and let someone else take care of your children. There are still problems from time to time, for instance when a child is sick, you have to do your best… It is useful to have good contacts with your friends, your neighbours. You are not unique for your children. And as time goes by, they grow up and everything becomes easier. …And eventually they are both adults, one of them has a job, and the other is specialising in medicine. One even told me "Mum, you don't have to worry, you weren't always there but I think it's very good, you have had a job you felt passionate about."

Do you think that a woman has to work more than a man to reach the same level in her career or to get as much consideration?

I do not think she has to work more than a man, but people are less likely to forgive her mistakes, they are more demanding. A woman also has to face different priorities. She has to make life choices and it is possible that she will not be fully committed to her job the same way a man is. If a woman gets scientifically involved and does a good job, I think her work will be appreciated.

And in your case, did your gender change anything?

No. It is possible that it is in fact the reason I was not given a position as a professor. And I know I will never be a "Professeur ordinaire". There was a time of restriction and it was obvious that, when someone from the lab had to be appointed, it was the young family man who got the promotion, and not the woman married to someone who was already tenured. Maybe I was disadvantaged because I was working with my husband, in the same team. But it is also true that I voluntarily stepped aside and did not fight. If I had wanted to fight, I could have made it, but I did not. I told myself "No, all in all, so-and-so is equally qualified, so it would be just as good if he got it. I already have a secure position." Women probably too often have that type of attitude, which explains why they do not get the job. They are not pushy, they have a form of honesty that men do not have, or not to the same extent.[98]

This interview is taken from a book of eleven interviews, which is the result of a final year Masters degree in Anthropology, in which interviews were carried out with women working in the sciences (exact and applied) in the five major universities of the French part of

[98] The interview is taken from Emilie Faes and Martine Jaminon, *Femmes de science belges: onze vies d'enthousiasme* (Belgian Women in Science: Eleven Lives of Enthusiasm), (Paris: L'Harmattan, Coll. Des idées et des femmes, 2003).

Belgium. Martine Jaminon rewrote the interviews, which were read by the interviewees themselves.

Assignment
Opening the discussion
> ➢ Can you cite the name of five women scientists? Can you tell in which field of sciences they were talented?
> ➢ Can you cite the name of five men scientists? Can you tell in which field of sciences they were talented?
> ➢ Can you name five women writers instead of scientists? Is there any difference in the answers?
> ➢ To what kind of job may studies in physics, mathematics, geography, biology, chemistry lead?

Questions about the Interview
> ➢ Does the interviewee speak about the rewards of a scientific career?
> ➢ Were women scientists influenced by someone specific (parents, teachers, partners) in the choice for a scientific career?
> ➢ Did they have any female role models that influenced their choice?
> ➢ Does she speak about the negative aspects of a job in scientific research? For instance, does she mention difficulties in managing private and professional lives? What type of difficulties does she describe? Is there any difference with other high level positions?
> ➢ Does the interview show awareness of gender discrimination whenever a woman tries to reach a higher-level position? (See C. Wennerås et A. Wold for additional information on gender discrimination).
> ➢ Do questioned women realise that there is a problem? Do they feel they have been discriminated? Does the interview indicate hestiance or ambiguity by changing answers (first a negative answer corrected into an affirmative answer?). (See interview with N. Dewandre for comparisons).
> ➢ According to the interviewed woman, what are the required qualities of a researcher? What makes someone unsuitable for

a career in science? What are the required qualities of a secretary? What makes someone unsuitable as a secretary? How do you estimate your own qualities?

➤ Would you describe the career of this woman as linear? Do you see interaction between life-cycle and professional trajectories? Do you find them interesting?

➤ Do you see whether women evaluate the autonomy in a high-level scientific job? Does she speak about the fact that it requires a quite important personal investment, leading to a timetable that is sometimes quite busy? Does she speak about a certain degree of freedom to do a part of the work at home, giving some freedom for children education?

➤ Does the interview speak about the importance of networks? One knows that effective networking is vital to a scientific community. Unfortunately, many scientific networks are typically and sometimes exclusionary male. Can you see trace of this in the interview?

Questions About Policies to Improve the Participation of Women

➤ Women's presence in science is rare. Does the interview show that women are aware of this fact? What are the reasons for this lack of women that are suggested by Nicole Dewandre? Can you find the reasons given by Nicole Dewandre for this inequality in the interview? Can one find these reasons in the other interviews and life stories? Are there other reasons given in these interviews? Could you suggest other reasons?

➤ Does the questioned woman agree with the positive measures mentioned in the Dewandre interview? Does she participate in them? Does she profit from them or does she think they are harmful?

Questions for Comparison

➤ What is the proportion of women researchers in the academic staff of your school (see Women and Science in Europe)?

➤ What is the proportion of women in the industrial staff of the field you are interested in (see database Strata)?

➤ Can you find data that compare gender ratios in Europe, Asia, United States, Africa?

Further Reading

Interview with Nicole DEWANDRE, Women and Sciences Unit, Research General Direction, European Commission.[99]

Reading this interview along with other material from the EU will allow students to get acquainted with the definition of the European Policy in terms of women in science, and to think about questions such as why women are so poorly involved in research, and what measures are being done to improve this situation and to help women reach higher academic or manager levels. Attention to the importance of integrating the gender dimension in scientific research, especially in medicine, sociology and economy, and the development of Women's and Gender Studies, is a real research field. Positive actions that should be supported by the EU policy include the setting-up of female scientific networks, the establishment of quota and targets, the development of role models and mentoring, the establishment of earmarked chairs, research funds and prizes for women scientists.

C. Wennerås et A. Wold, "Nepotism and Sexism in Peer-Review," *Nature* **(1997).**
This article shows that a woman has to publish 2.6 times more than a man to be recognised as having the same competence level.

Women in Industrial Research, A Wake-up Call for European Industry. Report to the European Commission from the High level Expert Group on Women in Industrial Research for Strategic Analysis of Specific Science and Technology Policy Issues (STRATA)

National Policies on Women and Science in Europe. The Helsinki Group on Women in Science, 2002

Database: www.ada-online.be/fr/6/index6.htm

---

[99] The opinions expressed in this article are those of the authors and do not necessarily reflect those of the European Commission.

PART III – TEACHING EXPERIENCES

Introduction

In this section of the book we have collected articles that describe the experience of teaching with memories in different classrooms. The Women's Studies experts who report on this format teach in diverse forms of education. Some teach in international contexts and have to address the different backgrounds of students. Others teach in interdisciplinary contexts where students with different expertise meet. From the descriptions, it is clear that the use of a form of foremother assignment can be used in many different contexts. Writing a life story about a foremother may help advanced history students to reflect upon the theoretical and methodological underpinnings of their discipline, but it may also be of help to students in professional training to reflect upon the issue of gender in their professions. What is also important for Women's Studies is that the assignment can be used in both formal education within universities and in training colleges, but that it is also applicable in the context of on-going education and public events. The assignment may be offered by a Women's Studies centre as a project for women in a city or region, or with a shared history. Or it may be part of public events, such as the celebration of a city or organisation. The examples in this section give an impression of the wide variety of possibilities. In all these instances, the foremother assignment will help students to become authors and will enhance reflection on the gendered nature of narratives and memories, thus providing students and researchers with a fresh perspective on history.

1. **'Her Present is my Past' – Teaching with Memories in Women's Studies Summer Schools**
    Andrea Pető and Berteke Waaldijk

Illustration: Photo of the NOISE Summer School in Antwerp (2003)

The Context

As we described in our Introduction, the foremother assignment has been incorporated in several NOISE Summer Schools since 1993. In 1994, an expanded and revised version of the assignment to write about a woman who could be described as a foremother, was integrated into the 'History Cluster' of the NOISE Summer School, which took place in Bologna.[100] The focus of the assignment was on clothing: students were asked to describe what their 'foremother' would be wearing, who had produced the textiles, who had stitched it together, who washed it, and what cultural meanings were attached to different dress codes. In 1996 and in 1999, the NOISE Summer School was located in Utrecht, and many students and faculty, who had known each other through the ATHENA Socrates Network, were involved. Here, the authors of this article have, with Joanna de Groot, Margarita Birriel and Maria Grever, revised the assignment again and tried it with groups of students who came from a range of different countries, and whose background and knowledge about women's history differed widely. The most recent experiment was undertaken in Antwerp in the NOISE Summer School in 2003, where students produced a collection of websites and a 'real' exposition that visualised the histories and memories of their foremothers.

---

[100] In this summer school, the History Cluster was formed by Jane Rendall, Joanna de Groot, Lucia Ferrante, Francoise Basch and Berteke Waaldijk.

Here we describe how the assignment has been used in the different summer schools, and reflect on our experiences with the format in the specific context of teaching with memories in a European summer school. About 50 students attended this summer school, and the teaching was done by an international team. The NOISE summer schools have one theme, which connects two or three clusters that address that theme from the perspective of a specific discipline. The foremother assignment was always part of the 'History Cluster', but cooperation with other clusters also happened. In 1996, for example, students discussed novels their foremothers had read in the 'literary studies cluster'. Students received the assignment and the reading material two months before the summer school started, and were expected to prepare their attendance by doing assignments, reading and collecting material.

Assignment

In 1999, the 'History Cluster' was part of the NOISE Summer School that had as its title 'Diasporic Identities and Mediated Cultures'. The cluster wanted to address historical dimensions of feminist reflections on this topic. We cite the Introduction to the 'History Cluster':

> Migration and Diaspora have been of great importance in European history. Firstly it is impossible to point to one European country that has not been influenced deeply by the experience of national and international migration [...]. Secondly the impact of European imperialism has caused many forms of voluntary and compulsory global migration that are typical of modern world history. Some histories of migration and Diaspora are forgotten and neglected, others are famous and are being told over and over again in history books and in popular culture. All those histories, whether famous or forgotten, contribute to different identities and cultures: they mediate feelings of belonging and marginality, they create national inclusion and exclusion. They are crucial in our understanding of multiculturalism as a result of the interaction between gender, ethnicity and class. Historical scholarship has two things to offer to feminists who address

multiculturalism as an issue that involves identities of migration and Diaspora: specific historical knowledge about global, national and local developments that resulted in unequal power relations [...] and understanding how official and unofficial historical knowledge, organized memory and personal recollections, national histories and private memories interact in constructing different identities, different senses of belonging and exclusion, *empowerment and marginalization.*[101]

The three days of the programme were devoted to, respectively: 'Connecting histories of women to general histories' (day 1), 'the interaction between private memories and public narratives' (day 2), and 'The organization of history and memory – the feminist challenge' (day 3). Students had to prepare for the work on the foremother-assignment by finding out as much as possible about the 'life of a woman who was alive and more or less grown-up in the year 1949'. This could be a personal relative (mother, grandmother, aunt), or a friend, or a public figure. Students had to bring to class a one-page description of the life of this woman, paying attention to nationality, class, ethnicity, education, experiences with migration, and a short description of the way she lived in 1949. The one-page texts were then copied and made into a booklet at the beginning of the summer school. Students were told that they could protect the privacy of the women they described by changing names or dates.

For the first day ('Connecting histories of women to general histories'), the students had to prepare for an on-line discussion about experiences of their 'foremother' within contexts of nationalism, racism, ethnic repression, migration, poverty or wealth. They were asked to think about whether the life of the foremother would shed new light on 'big histories of imperialism, dictatorship and multiculturalism', whether there are parts of her life that were 'famous or forgotten', and what may have caused fame or invisibility. The next part of the assignment asked the students to compare their own life with that of their foremother, to reflect upon the sources that were

[101] Brirriel, De Groot, Andrea Pető and Berteke Waaldijk, "Cluster II-Women's History" in *NOISE Summer Sschool Programme-Book.*

available to acquire knowledge about her (either official sources like books, newspapers, national archives, or unofficial ones, such as personal stories, family secrets, gossip). We asked the students to think about the ways in which the woman could be part of a history – how could her life be part of a national history – and if they could envisage a history about all women in 1949.

For the second day ('Interaction between private memories and public narratives'), the students had to prepare for an in-class discussion of the way their foremother related to the national state where she lived in 1949. So, for instance: was she a citizen? What were her rights? Was she supported in any way by the state or prosecuted? Did she have nationalist feelings or did she participate in transitions that took place? The second set of questions asked students to think about the cultural identity of their foremother: what forms of culture did she participate in (books, films, music, fashion, consumer cultures etc.), and whether these forms of culture were nationally or ethnically connoted? Students were invited to collect material that might help to understand the connections between popular culture and personal memories.

The session on the third day ('Organization of history and memory') took place at the IIAV where students were invited to search, in the rich collections of this library, for information that might shed light on the life of the foremothers. Students then had to discuss the way the politics of memory worked and what information should be collected to write about the histories of their foremothers.

Two optional extra assignments allowed students (1) to explore theoretical writing about history and memory, and (2) to make a website about their foremother. Scanning and website building instructions and support were available. In 2003, most of this assignment was used again, but the year was changed to 1953, and the last assignment (website) was expanded: all students were to make an exhibition about their foremother, either a virtual exhibition on-line, or a real exhibition that could be visited. This turned out to have a great impact. Students were extremely active and ambitious in creating exhibitions, on-line or in a specifically designed space.

Reflections

Several interesting points can be made about these teaching experiences. The first point that struck us as teachers was the choice of foremothers. The assignment was formulated in such a way that the students were free to choose a woman from their personal history (family or close friend), or a woman they knew through her public role (a politician, a cultural hero, such as a film star, a novelist, or a feminist). Almost all students in the 1999 NOISE Summer School chose a woman to whom they were 'privately' related. None recognised 1949 as the publishing date of the most influential work by Simone de Beauvoir. The assignment seems to help to overcome not only the South-North, but also the East-West division, and, thus, to break away from the semiotic burden of the Cold War. Both in the 1999 summer school in Utrecht and in the different oral history workshops Andrea Pető organised in former communist countries, the large majority of women chose a kinship-foremother, mostly grandmothers, as foremothers. The East and West or South and North division became meaningless, since the general lack of women in public, eligible for foremother status, is a world-wide phenomenon. In the history textbooks there are very few women with whom readers might identify, because most of them are either heroines or victims of violence. The symbolic space available for women in public is often related to misery and suffering. The 'great ladies' who are visible are characterised by loneliness and they have servants, not students.[102] Surprisingly, these great ladies, such as Kolontaj, Luxemburg, and Zetkin, are those who were remembered as exceptions by students who came from former Soviet-countries, which is related to the hierarchical character of remembering in these countries.[103]

The second point we want to make is that the decision to vary the format the students could use to present their knowledge about

[102] See Andrea Pető, "Images and Phantasien. Europas Töchter und 'Damen' in der Vergangenheit" in Silke Roth, Ingrid Miethe, Leske-Budrich, (eds.), *Europas Töchter. Traditionen, Erwartungen und Strategien von Frauenbewegungen in Europa*. (The Daughters of Europe. Expectations and Strategies of the European Women's Movements), (2003), 21-31. The confererence was organised by Evangaelischen Akademie Thueringien, Boell Stiftung, Ost-West Europaeischen Frauennetzwerkes. The conference also organised a collective foremother exercise.

[103] Andrea Pető, "Memory Unchanged. Redefinition of Identities in Post WWII Hungary," in Eszter Andor, Andrea Pető, Istvan György Tóth, (eds.), *CEU History Department Yearbook 1997-98* (Budapest, 1999), 135-153.

foremothers has proven to be a very fortunate one. The written paper, the classroom discussions, the lectures (where teachers could refer to foremother stories) and digital discussions, and, in 2003, the exhibition, allowed students different voices. In 1999, the format of on-line discussion proved to be very effective in adding different hierarchies. Some students, who had been silent in classroom discussions, posted great contributions to the bulletin board, and this offered them a different type of visibility and a different level of identification.[104] Apparently we strengthened the authority of the students by using different formats. The explicit instruction – to be prepared to learn from others – motivated students to ask questions of fellow students as well as of teachers. The somewhat more anonymous format (although all students knew with whom they were talking) of on-line discussions have also contributed to the students' ability to speak about very painful and traumatic experiences. In 2003, the difference between on-line discussions and classroom discussions was smaller, which may be the result of growing familiarity of students with chatting and on-line real-time communication. However, this aspect of communication in an educational context certainly deserves closer attention, and may be explored more in the future. In this context, it is crucial to think of better and more accessible ways to keep the records of all that happened (oral, printed and digital communications) in the teaching situations where the assignments are used.

With regard to the contents of the discussions, we noticed that the displacement of experiences and memories on to the lives of other women – foremothers – was extremely productive in bringing sensitive and painful memories into the classroom. Some space may be created for 'the other woman', the foremother, where students can maintain some distance. This has, in our experience, allowed students to talk about serious issues like deportation and genocide, that would have been too difficult to address un-mediated. Asking them to tell the story of a woman allows them to differentiate between the private story and the massiveness of a national history of violence. For example, writing about one German and one Dutch woman and their experiences of the Second World War, or about one Hungarian and

---

[104] We used WebCT. We now regret that the files of this discussion have not been kept.

123

one Russian woman's experiences of Stalinism makes conversations possible where a confrontation between national histories would have silenced the students. In addition to this basic element in foremother assignments, it proved very helpful for the interaction among students to focus on one year in European history. Comparative perspectives were almost inescapable when students told each other, as specialists, about their foremother, how she had lived in a specific year, and how this differed from other experiences. The year 1949 was very effective with the echoes of the Second World War, the Cold War, and decolonisation, but when 1953 was chosen, the same active multi-faceted comparative interaction happened. All students, thus, contributed to the shared need for multi-voiced histories.

The introduction of the history of women's movements, was a topic that made students aware of just how lopsided many women's histories are. Knowledge available about women's movements in the USA and Western Europe is overwhelming. But for some other countries this is less the case. When teaching women's history to an international group of students, there is a real risk that the specific knowledge about some western countries will become the measuring stick. By asking explicitly for the students to find information about the emancipation of women in their own country, the knowledge about the history of feminism and women's movements can become substantially diversified.[105]

In this short description we hope to have given an indication of how incredibly effective teaching with memories can be in an international group. It enhances comparative perspectives, stimulates a lively sense of the diversity of European Women's history and, most of all, provides a real empowerment of students *vis-à-vis* European history. For a more theoretically elaborated reflection, we refer to the introduction in this book.

---

[105]Karen Offen, *European Feminisms. A Political History 1700-1950*, (Stanford UP, 2000); Bonnie Smith, *The Gender of History. Men, Women and Historical Practices*, (Harvard UP, 1998).

2. "All the Countries of our Foremothers Were Colonised by Russians except Yugoslavia"[106]
Andrea Pető

Illustration: The Soviet Army is Greeted by the People
(Historical Museum, Blagoevgrad)

Introduction

The title sentence was written by Ziva, a student of mine, as a comment on imperialism in the chat-room we are using in our course at the Central European University (Budapest). It illustrates well the issues I would like to address in this paper related to empire and memory. The course, 'Historical Frames of Identity and Locating Women's Memories in History' is a result of our common work with

---

[106] I am grateful to Ana, Ziva, Ljuba, Ieva, Ewa, Eniko, Redi, Michaela and Aida for their comments and for the inspiration I got from our common work, which made the writing of this article possible. Thanks to Anikó Balogh for the web support, and to Marina Mogilner and Ilia Gerasimov for their comments on an earlier version of this text.

125

Berteke Waaldijk,[107] in which we use the format of the foremother assignment to understand the politics of gendered remembering, alongside analysing history textbooks, exhibitions, and through women's life stories. Besides reading the standard texts on memory, women's memory, on politics of exhibition and empires,[108] the students are expected to make a web-site of their own where they not only place the texts of different assignments, but make a virtual museum for their foremothers. Berteke Waaldijk was teaching the course in Utrecht in the Winter Term of 2003-2004 for Dutch undergraduates in Dutch, while I was teaching the course for Slovak, Croat, Bosnian, Hungarian, Lithuanian, Estonian, Slovenian, Moldavian, and Polish post-graduate students in English in Budapest. In the last class of the term, I gave them the draft of this paper, so I am also using their comments as well as the transcripts from the chat sessions.

For this educational occasion in Budapest, I modified the time-frame of the foremother assignment, which was set in the 1950s,[109] a time in Eastern European history when the imperial narrative – the history of the Soviet Empire – is the dominant meta-narrative. The main characteristic of the historiography about the 1950s is the fascination by individuals, as agents of history, without asking the main structural questions about collaboration, accommodation and

---

[107] On the module's history and results, see Berteke Waaldijk, Andrea Pető, "Writing the Lives of Foremothers. The History and Future of a Feminist Teaching Tool," in Rosi Braidotti, Janny Niebert, Sanne Hirs (eds.), *The Making of the European Women's Studies* Vol. IV. (Utrecht, 2002), 149-162.
see http://www.let.uu.nl/womens_studies/summerschool2003/programme.html or
http://www.ceu.hu/gend/Peto/index.htm

[108]The readings were: Anne McClintock, "Soft-Soaping Empire. Commodity Racism and Imperial Advertising," (*idem., Imperial Leather: Race, Gender, and Sexuality in the Colonial Contest*, (Routledge, 1995) in *The Visual Culture Reader*; Berteke Waaldijk, "Colonial Constructions of a Dutch Women's Movement: 1898," in K. Rottcher, *et.al.* (eds.) *Differenzen in de Geschlechterdifferenz*; Mitchell, T., "Orientalism and the Exhibitionary Order," in *The Visual Culture Reader*, 217-236, Paul Greenhalgh, "Education, Entertainment and Politics: Lessons from the Great International Exhibitions," in Peter Vergo (ed.), *The New Museology*, (1989), 74-98.

[109] The assignment is the following: Find out as much as possible about the life of a woman who was alive and more or less grown-up in the 1950s. This may be a relative (grandmother, aunt), a friend or somebody who was a public figure in your country. I advise you to find someone who matters to you personally, this may be either as a political or intellectual inspiration, or a person you know or are related to. I will refer to this woman as the 'foremother', but she should not necessarily be a family-relation.

126

resistance; nor is there any understanding of the ways in which remembering is constructed today about that historical period. Historians are usually fascinated by the individual life stories of the Party nomenclature, or the *stakhanovites*, or listing the individual losses and sufferings, without determining a wider conceptual framework of historical analyses, which would examine how the Empire was constructed. During our work, I was interested in trying to "re-write conditions of impossibility" into "conditions of possibility".[110]

The question for me was what kind of memories we have about the Empire, or how the Empire determines how it is remembered. Narrating imperial experience is a constant struggle with the impossibility to speak, in the conditions of impossibility, while a web of silences, absences and presences are here to struggle. I was curious to see how all these female students of Gender Studies from the former Soviet Block, who are more political than 'average' students,[111] relate themselves to the memories and experiences of their foremothers. It was also a part of the study to investigate the available "cultural repertoire" (Lamont) to relate ourselves to our pasts. Pluralities of historical experience are needed to palimpsest complexities of experiences and their representation.

But my label about the enrolled students as being 'more political' made Michaela write the following comment in the first version of this paper: "concerning the 'more political' I would really doubt, maybe gender sensitive would be better? I cannot assert that the answers we provided in class could be referred to as more political, on the contrary we avoided to be political", which reflects on the self-imposed borders of historical understanding.

Teaching with Chatting
During the classes, I thought it was not difficult to critically summarise the arguments of the required readings, nor to chat about

---

[110] Gayatri Spivak, *A Critique of Postcolonial Reason: Toward History of the Vanishing Present*, (Harvard UP, 1999), 272.

[111] Their political commitment is illustrated by the fact that most of the students performed the *Vagina Monologues* on Valentine's Day when the CEU administration put red boxes with red-heart-stamped papers encouraging male students to send valentine greetings to female students and *vice versa*, in an educational institution for students coming mostly from the former Soviet Block countries without a Valentine culture.

the everyday experiences of the foremothers of the 1950s. But it turned out I was wrong, as Redi inserted a different opinion:

> I actually found this VERY difficult since I didn't feel I knew enough about my foremother. My knowledge was mostly based on the information I received from the newspapers and articles in the journals and we all know how biased and one-sided these stories can be. So actually it was very difficult to move beyond the typical constructions of a woman's life story and sort of try to see what her everyday experience 'really' might have been in the 1950s. Thus, I often felt I didn't manage to reconstruct the story as I simply didn't have enough background knowledge.

But I felt it was difficult to frame the individual life stories in the wider framework of the big narratives of history-writing, such as imperialism, colonialism, etc. As far as methodology is concerned, we used not only classroom discussion, but also a chat-room for discussion as well as analysing and reflecting on the assignments written by other students. So, to illustrate my point in this paper – namely our unchangeable character of constructing the memory of the empire – I will use quotations from a chat-room transcript from the class of 3 March, 2004, when we discussed the issue of empire, colonialism and gender. Aida wrote this as a summary for our discussion:

> All of the stories involve migration as a means of survival on the one hand, or as a method of extermination, that is the forced migration to concentration camps or prisons. It is interesting to note that all of the countries (even those who were the colonisers at some point of the time) were oppressed by other countries, so our foremothers came exactly from that milieu. I would say that the common feature of most of the texts is the imperialism or any other oppressive force that has had pretty much the same methods and impacts in different time periods, but not only in the terms how the colonisers were treating their

subject, but also the experiences that those women had. They could be said to have been experiencing pretty similar destinies.

This comment caused serious influx of comments, but they all agreed with Redi's comment: "I would emphasise once more that the experience with imperialism would be a common thread between these stories of foremothers, even if they were not directly persecuted under the expanding soviet regime, they were still influenced by the 'realities' of their countries", or with the comment from Michaela: "the greatest majority of the foremothers experience the expansion of the Soviet regime".

In the chat discussion, Ieva and Eniko underlined that their countries were small and not imperialistic at all, and that they did not have any imperial experience. In the case of Hungary, as Eniko put it about her foremother, who was brought up in the Soviet Union and married to a Polish actor, the 'Hungarian' experience is "different from the coloniser experience", arguing with difference.

It was most interesting to see how Michaela's remark that the guards in the *gulag* of her foremother were Lithuanians made Ieva blush, as if she were there. Later on, reading the first draft of this text, Ieva inserted:

> Yes, I did feel uneasy after Michaela's statement (however I kept silent) and I think I took it kind of personally, because I felt like I hear the accusation to the nation which I consider myself belonging to. But it's the same like Lithuanians (or Moldavians) might associate Russian nation with oppressors/aggressors/enemy. It is a very familiar feeling to me and I'm sure - to many ex-USSR nations/people. Andrea after that commented, and I agree with her, that we have to see further and have in mind the whole situation of the war, where the oppressive forces can easily turn people against each other within the system, and you can no longer think in terms of which nation is killing which. All those nations were subjected to the working of larger imperialist forces.

But Michaela commented on the manuscript: "I don't remember that my words had such a reaction. On the contrary, the conclusion that we came up with was that these nations were used and manipulated by the entire system".

This episode indicates that this 'imagined' national frame could offer protection for the individual. As Michaela underlined, "the Russian language imposed culture and politics". So, the comments introduced a total lack of agency. Ana and Ziva advocated for Yugoslavia as an exception where, "imperialism as a frame" does not apply, while Aida, coming from a Protectorate, just quietly smiled, without saying a word. So, in an emotional moment, I dared to add to the chat-room, the "colonial experience is what the others have", referring to the shameful identification, for example, with the Balkans, to which it is always the neighbouring country that belongs, not 'us'. Thus, for me, the question was how is it that we were all able to recognise the individual suffering, but not the factors causing it and the collective attempts to avoid suffering from the imperial structures.

The History of Memory of an Empire: Unconnectedness
The aim of the course was to understand the politics of gendered remembering. The course gives an understanding of how different forms of media (textbooks, exhibitions, photographs) work to construct the frames of remembering, and how we want to, or are able to, remember women living in the 1950s in our countries.[112] During the class, I was astonished by the apolitical character of remembering about the foremothers, as if the Soviet Empire did not exist at all, or as if the Empire did not have a wider meaning influencing all different structures of life. The only exception was the Moldavian story, which was structured by suffering. Thus, in what follows, I will list briefly some of the factors which I believe have led to the unconnectedness of gendered remembering of the Empire.

---

[112] The readings for this topic were: Gianna Pomata, "History, Particular and Universal: Some Recent Women's History Textbooks." *Feminist Studies*, Vol. 19, No. 1, (Spring 1993), 7-50; Andrea Pető, "A Missing Piece? How Women in the Communist Nomenclature are not Remembering." *East European Politics and Society*, Vol.. 16, No. 3, (Fall 2003), 948-958; Berteke Waaldijk, "Of Stories and Sources, Feminist History," in Rosemarie Buikema and Anneke Smelik, (eds.), *Women's Studies and Culture, A Feminist Introduction*, (London: ZED-books, 1995), 14-25; Maria Grever, "The Pantheon of Feminist Culture: Women's Movements and the Organization of Memory." *Gender History*, Vol. 9, No. 2, 364-374.

Our historical memory is constructed in a chronological line. The stories of the nation, the acts of people are elaborated in the genre of the chronicle, where the topics are embedded in the universal context. Events of life are arranged around the hero of the age, usually the ruler or, in our case, the assignment of a Communist Party Secretary who determines the framed narrative of the past. Since the late Renaissance, artists have also expressed the lasting effect of historical events or the deeds of great historical figures. In other words, they showed bygone events, not merely reproductively, but also interpretatively, as they had a constructed meaning for their contemporaries. Therefore, histories are given allegorical meanings apart from the obvious schemes. The allegory, the metaphor became a tool of interpreting the historical significance of the given event, but to uncover the symbolic meaning, a consensus was needed among the readers and the viewers. The 'oppression by the empire' is a powerful metaphor used in order to construct an interpretative frame for writing about events in the past.

The memory of great personalities glorified already in their lifetimes or upon their death was also perpetuated by the tools of art, ranging from illustrated collections of works to our foremother stories in the class. Past events became the basis for inspiring future political acts; heroes of the past became regularly present in political speeches as good examples for the future. The stereotypical male virtues and some female heroes became more and more frequent. The pictorial cliché of, for instance, the 'Hungarian man' or 'Croatian woman', contributed to the popularisation and reception of these ideas from the nineteenth century. Women made a remarkable path: no longer as goddesses of the heart, but also the repositories of national life, patriotism, autonomous national identity as our foremothers became 'examples' for that particular country. The sensitivity of women, speaking strictly about daughters and wives, became the source and perpetrators of national feeling for the fathers, brothers, and husbands.

The representation of passion, like suffering or oppression, is used for constructing imagined communities like nations. The aim of construction of this frame is not merely to conjure up the martyrs of the nation, but to urge for historical justice via their evocation, to show up justice in history in the moral sense in the hopefully very near future. This passion can be a desire for independence, hate for the coloniser, or hope to eliminate oppression. This genre is necessarily tragic, with its utopian character. The dominating agents of remembering are constructed as positive, ascending, glorious narratives. The personification of virtues, geniuses all allude, beyond the unique historical event, to their presumed moral meaning. So our foremothers were representing for us the virtue of suffering and individual success stories. As Enikő put it, "I did not have the intention to write the story of my foremother with a moral, however, if it turned out that way, that may be because the sources I used contained information from which it was easy to construct a success or a victim narrative".

Historical remembrance is normally attached to venues of triumphant or lost battles and the death of heroes. In nearly every town and in many villages, columns exist, memorial tablets commemorate the local heroes or great sons of the place. It is very rarely done with statues of great daughters. I was deeply shocked when, during the introductory class, Ziva said that she never saw any exhibition about women's pasts, at least not in Eastern Europe, and not in her home country. She added later to the manuscript, "[it is] because I don't like history and I usually visit museums when I visit some other countries. This is the reason I saw the exhibitions of women in New York, Alice Springs, and in Vanuatu".

The objectified works of historical memory populating the streets and squares warn us that the real spaces of our everyday existence are, at the same time, symbolic spaces as the imaginary realm of history becomes embodied in the monuments. The commemorative statues constitute a part of social publicity representing the attitude of the elite to history; they may also fall victim to change in the political set-up. Monuments with metaphoric representation of women replaced the statues of heroic Soviet soldiers. As recognised in the class, we found very few common elements of our historical imaginary, beyond feelings of being oppressed and colonised.

The anti-historicism of modernism, however, offered new possibilities for constructing frames of historical remembering and, unfortunately, the same traps. The anti-historicism declined to follow the old models, rejected the so-called traditional evocations of the past, and basically the representation of history as an ideal reality, the allegorisation of history. The anti-historicism was very appropriate for the purpose of new social movements, like women's movements, which, themselves, are struggling with a lack of history and historical predecessors. This is one of the reasons why the question of which political force has appropriated women's day and the memory of women's political activism was discussed. So, the past on display has deliberately fixed eyes on the future, ignoring enfeebled traditions, and creating the work of remembering.

Others picked up objects from the sunken collective past, which they converted into parts of their internal, personal worlds. This latter strategy was followed in the assignment. Apart from being personal, the view of history is also fragmentary, precisely on account of its distance from the collective images of the past. The 'collective narrative' has lost it validity; its surviving enigmatic torso acquired new values in the course of elaboration. In the nineteenth century, history provided the scenery against which artistic imagination was set; today, history can claim that it is only art that can links the present to the past, which is known only by fragments. Hegemonic reconstruction is no longer possible, at least for a long period of time, but if an attempt is made, it can only be personal and individualistic, such as in the case of our foremothers. It turned out that individual life stories offer the only "site for remembering", to use Pierre Nora's term for remembering, but within its limitations.

Conclusions

The stories of the foremothers in our class are all tragic stories: forced migration, discrimination by ethnicity and by gender. But as Ewa put it, "I wouldn't be so pessimistic, besides, to a certain extent, the stories were responses to the assignments' requirements, and also we have to take into consideration that particular period".

The participants of the class were taking strength or, to use the terminology of the 1970s women's movement, empowerment by their strength and survival strategies. They all admired the life achievements of their foremothers, which inspired them to make rich and colourful web pages. I feel we took the first step together on the long way towards understanding structures of power. However, in the case of the assignment to write the life stories of identification, victimisation or resistance, we surprisingly found that the victimised narratives were more convincing than either the stories of resistance or the stories of identification. As Enikő inserted into the draft of an article I gave to the class to read: "This says something about us or maybe about how we learned to think of historiography".

In the foremother stories, the structures of oppression remained unseen. Miglena Nikolchina pointed out in her article, one of the reasons why there is no women's movement in post-1989 Eastern Europe, which might help us to explain unconnectedness. During the 'statist feminist' period, no matter that nearly all women worked, which enabled them to experience economic freedom and a certain autonomy, they failed to connect the experience of discrimination, the glass ceiling with an understanding of the patriarchal structures.[113] That individual survival strategy, which was part of the emancipation policy of the Soviet Block, offered a framework of non-confrontation with the main structural elements of the political system.

This is part of our common heritage from the Empire. We are all blind to the structures of oppression as a result of how they were used by the Empire as a discursive technique for normalisation, and we are hoping to find refuge in individualism and in a nation-statehood frame of remembering as the only sites that remained for us as sites of remembering. But that is a doomed enterprise from the beginning. Does the Empire strike back? (Even with this article?)

Bibliography

Magdolna Láczay Dr. ed. *Nők és férfiak, avagy a nemek története.* **(Men and Women, or Gender History)** *Rendi társadalompolgári társadalom a 16. században.* **Nyíregyháza: Nyíregyházi Főiskola Gazdaságtudományi Kar, 2003. (Hungarian)**

Andrea Pető ed. *Társadalmi nemek képe és emlékezete Magyarországon a 19.-20. században.* **(The Gendered Image and Representation in Hungary in Nineteenth and Twentieth Centuries.) Budapest: Nők a Valódi**

---

[113] Nikolchina, Miglena, "The Seminar: Mode d'emploi. Impure Spaces in the Light of Late Totalitarianism." *Differences* Vol. 15, No. 1, (2002), 96-127.

Esélyegyenlőségért Alapítvány, 2003. (In Hungarian). The most recent collection of research on gender history in Hungary. The books are based on conference presentations.

Andrea Pető. *Hungarian Women in Politics 1945-1951*. **New York: Columbia UP, 2003.**
A comprehensive monograph covering the history of women's activism describing the process how the rich world of the Hungarian women's associations were destroyed. The book also consists of photographs and an annotated index.

Andrea Pető and Béla Rásky eds. *Construction and Reconstruction. Women, Family and Politics in Central Europe 1945-1998.* **Budapest: CEU, The Programme on Gender and Culture, Austrian Science and Research Liaison Office, Budapest, OSI Network Women's Programme, 1999.**A collection of essays by Hungarian and Austrian historians and sociologists covering the issues of family policy, regulation of abortion, gendered representations in films, feminist genealogies during statist feminism.

The webpage of the Esther's Bag, the Hungarian Jewish Women's organisation offers readings on Untold Stories of women and on reconceptualising gender and judaism. http://www.nextwave.hu/esztertaska A selected list of institutions and contact persons active in the research and teaching of Gender Studies. The site also offers access to different databases and ongoing research projects.

www.tarki.hu look for subsection: "Női Adattár" (Data on Women) Information on employment and Women's Studies: The Impact of Women's Studies Training on Women's Employment in Europe. www.hull.ac.uk/ewsi

3 Foremothers Between Margin and Centre. Writing Life Stories in a Class on Women's History and Women's Literature
Berteke Waaldijk

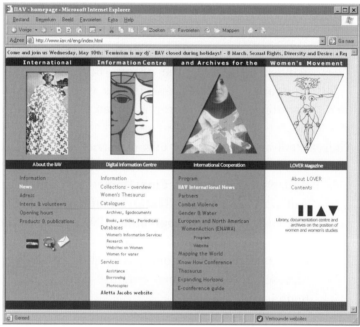

Illustration: The International Information Centre and Archives for the Women's Movement in Amsterdam is a treasure house for public and private memories of women (www.iiav.nl)

Background and Context

In 1987, at the Faculty of Arts at Utrecht University in the Netherlands, an interdisciplinary undergraduate programme in Women's Studies started. This programme allowed students from different disciplines to focus on Women's Studies for 1.5 years of their studies. The programme was the result of the work, in the preceding years, by students and teachers in different disciplines: literary studies, history, film studies, art history, and medieval studies. They had worked together unofficially.[114] The official recognition of the programme allowed for the development of new courses that reflected the

---

[114] The names of Mieke Bal, Fia Dieteren, Corrie Hoogetoorn, Els Kloek, Ria Lemaire, Maaike Meijer, Anne Claire Mulder, Jetty Schaap, Anneke Smelik and Corrie Verstoep should be mentioned as the pioneers in Women's Studies in the Arts at Utrecht University.

interdisciplinary interests of the staff. One of these new courses was called 'Between Margin and Centre, Women and Cultural Traditions', which dealt with women's literature and women's history.[115] The course explicitly addressed the interdisciplinary combinations of history and literary studies. Students read theoretical texts about the absence of women from literary histories, from national histories, and about the discussion on the existence of a separate women's cultural tradition.[116] They also learned about inclusion and exclusionary practices and the difficulty of 'restoring women to history'. Students were invited to think about non-hierarchical ways of combining historical and literary knowledge. In addition to the theoretical texts, they read 10 to 15 novels written by women, from different periods. Apart from five novels that were discussed extensively in class, students were free in the choice of those novels, and literary fame was not one of the requirements.[117]

The course has been taught every year from 1988 until the present. Approximately 150 students in the Women's Studies programme have taken this course, which is obligatory for Women's Studies majors. After a few years the title was changed from 'Between Margin and Centre, Women and Cultural Traditions' to 'Margin and Centre, Women and Cultural Innovation'.

The assignment was to write a paper about the life of a female ancestor, 'foremother' (in Dutch the word 'foremother' does not exist, although the word 'forefather' does). A visit to the IIAV, the Women's Library and Archives in Amsterdam, was an integrated part of the assignment.[118] One of the main aims of this assignment was to teach students about the different sources for writing women's history:

---

[115] Over the years, Berteke Waaldijk – a women's historian – has co-taught this course with colleagues with disciplinary backgrounds in literary studies: Anneke Smelik (1988-1990), Maaike Meijer (1991), Rosemarie Buikema (1992-1994), Agnes Andeweg (1995-1998), Paula Jordao (1999-2003). In 2004 Lotte Jensen taught the course.

[116] Carrol Smith-Rosenberg, "Politics and Culture in Women's History: A Symposium." *Feminist Studies*, 6.1 (1980), 26-49; Caroline Heilbrun, *Writing a Woman's Life*, (1988); Nancy Armstrong, "Literature as Women's History." *Genre XIX*, (Winter 1986), 347-369; Bonnie Smith, "On Writing Women's Work," in *EUI Working Paper* HEC No. 91/71.

[117] Although the titles of the five obligatory books differed from year to year, the following titles were regularly included: Christine de Pisan, *Cité des Dames*; Charlotte Brontë, *Jane Eyre*; Djuna Barnes, *Nightwood*, Toni Morrison, *Beloved*, and Clarice Lispector, *A hora da estrela*. Students were allowed to read the books in Dutch or in English translation.

[118] For more see the website www.iiav.nl

personal communications (memories of people who knew the woman described), primary sources (archival material, documents that have been kept by family and friends), secondary historical sources (history books and articles), and literary texts that were produced and consumed in the time the foremother lived. Thus, reflection on the many-faceted way knowledge about women's lives is produced became the central focus of the assignment.

Assignment[119]

The assignment consisted of 1) a rather free and broad general assignment that could be interpreted very liberally, and 2) some very specific questions that had to be answered in detail in an annex.

1. The assignment in general:

Choose a woman – you may be related through family or through other ties – the only requirement is that you will be able to gain some knowledge about her life through informal channels: via memories of people who knew her, or have heard about her, via privately owned objects, such as letters, diaries pieces of clothing or jewellery. The other condition is that she is, at this moment, no longer alive, and that she lived for the major part of the twentieth century. Try to reconstruct the life of this female 'foremother' in three different years: how she lived in 1900, in 1920, and in 1950. When reconstructing her life, focus on the main questions that are discussed in our course:

> ➢ In what cultural traditions and/or cultural innovations did she participate?
> ➢ In what ways was she included in or excluded from cultural practices?
> ➢ Would you describe parts of her life as belonging to a female cultural tradition?

Students had to provide all other students in the course with a copy of their foremother-biography (part 1), which was to be around 2500 words. The instructions stated that students were free to choose the style and the format, and that the biography could take the form of a

---

[119] For a discussion of the scholarly texts used in this class see the bibliography.

traditional academic paper, a short story, an interview or a newspaper article, a letter, or it could combine different genres. Confidentiality of the papers, as well as the discussion about them, was guaranteed: all promised not to discuss the personal aspects of the lives of the foremothers outside the classroom. The students were advised to start collecting material and information about their foremother's life immediately, to look for people they could talk with, to use letters, telephone conversations, family-visits and e-mail (only from 1996 onwards) to collect their material, and to start looking for material objects that might have survived.

2. The Annex
The biography was to have an annex (part 2), which consisted of the answers to a series of detailed questions that could only be answered after a visit to an archive and library. The visit to the International Information Centre and Archive of the Women's Movement (IIAV) provided the students with the opportunity to complete this part of the assignment. The teachers advised the students to start writing down crucial facts from their foremother's life before the visit to the IIAV, since this would help them to use the archives and library to their full potential.

Specific questions (to be answered in the annex):

> ➤ Make a list of thesaurus terms that will help you find information about your foremother. (For example, work, ethnicity, motherhood, cultural participation, living and housing, politics, citizenship, etc.)
> ➤ When you use these thesaurus terms, search for bibliographies, write down two full titles of bibliography that may contain helpful titles for your research. One of the titles should be available at the IIAV, one should be located outside the IIAV.
> ➤ Find three books, collections or archives that may contain biographical information that will help you to write the life of your foremother. (Please note this does have to be direct biographical information about your specific foremother: you can look for books (both scholarly and literary texts may be

useful) about women who lived in the same period, in the same class, in the same region).

➢ Find (again using the thesaurus terms) 5 titles of scholarly books or articles available at the IIAV that may contain information useful for your research about the life of your foremother. You could look for scholarly work on labour, ethnicity, motherhood, cultural participation, living and housing, politics, citizenship. Make notes about at least two of your findings and summarise them in your assignment or in the annex.

➢ Find two books that are not available at the IIAV, but that might contain information about the life of your foremother, either in general or more specifically. Find out where and how you might gain access to these books. Give the titles – you are not required to read these books for this assignment.

➢ Find the title (and if possible, look at a copy) of at least one journal or one novel that your foremother herself may have read in the different timeslots (1900 / 1920 / 1950).

➢ Find an archive-collection that might contain information about the type of life that your foremother led in the different timeslots. Give title and location of this collection and your argument for its possible usefulness.

➢ Find out whether any Women's Studies scholar at this moment is doing research that may pertain to the life of your foremother. Write down name, address and research topic.

➢ Find an image that may serve to illustrate your foremother research.

➢ Report about the answers to the questions in a separate annex. Describe difficulties and successes in collecting this information. You may also choose to integrate the answers in a recognisable form in the paper that contains the foremother's life story.

After students had researched their foremother's life and written the 'biography' or 'life story', the class (on average consisting of approximately 10-15 students) discussed these papers. All students read all life stories, and for every paper, two students prepared specific comments that compared the paper to other papers and that connected the life story to the themes that had been discussed in class.

Reflections on the Assignment [120]

Public and Private in the Classroom and in History

The students were not obliged to do so, but the majority of them did choose a maternal or paternal (great)-grandmother. The requirement that some information about the foremother should be collected via 'informal' contacts made it logical for students to use family-connections. Some opted for (great-) aunts, and they argued that, this way, they could study the life of a woman who was not married or did not have children. A few studied the life of a woman who was related to a friend, or who had been a friend of the family. Many students expressed the impact their research had on family relations: some families were honoured or flattered that someone who attended university paid attention to a woman from their family, while others were worried that private details about this person's life would be discussed by strangers. Some students had to promise not to write about certain facts in their papers, for example, an out-of-wedlock baby, work in a pub, adulterous love relations. The promise of confidentiality within the class was not always enough, and some students decided to provide some information only orally during the discussions.

This aspect of the assignment made students aware of different forms of knowledge; they too felt that it was a new experience to discuss in class the private life of someone who they considered as a private relation. Several students argued that they wanted to keep alive the memory of a beloved grandmother who had died, or they wrote about a curiosity they had felt about a certain woman in their family. This meant that in class we could discuss the way private and public knowledge differ.

The social background played a role in these perceptions as well. Students who chose a foremother from a lower class family had to

---

[120] Part of the following is taken from Berteke Waaldijk, "Yearning for Culture. Citizenship and the Humanities," (trans. Mischa Hoyinck and Robert Chesall) in Berteke Waaldijk, *Talen naar cultuur. Burgerschap en de Letterenstudies*, (Utrecht, 2005). The complete English version is available at http://www.let.uu.nl/~Berteke.Waaldijk/personal/

explain why this woman was 'worth' the attention bestowed on her. Students from families with an upper class background reported on being asked why they did not choose to write about women who were related to men who had played an important role in Dutch public life: "Why don't you write about your other grandmother? Her life was so much more interesting, she has been married to this famous artist".

Social mobility also became part of the discussions, with students recognising class differences between their foremothers, they reflected on their own position within a family history: "I am the first of our family to go to university, my grandmother would have been so proud of me".

Dutch Women's History
Traditionally, life stories of foremothers reflected Dutch women's history during the twentieth century: many foremothers were born in rural areas, and moved to a city at some time in their lives. Examples of women scholars, writers and entrepreneurs were rare, but the biographies were teeming with maidservants. Many grandmothers, great-grandmothers and great-aunts spent part of their lives as paid help in someone else's private domain: as nannies, housekeepers, and seamstresses. Some foremothers did not yearn for marriage – and this could lead to speculation of homosexuality – while other foremothers showed no interest in a career of paid work.[121] Several students described the lives of women who experienced colonial migration: fiancées who left for the colonies to work or to fight in colonial wars. The private side of colonial history in the Netherlands became palpable in stories about Indonesian housekeepers who got pregnant by their Dutch employers and who lost their child to his family.[122] It became apparent how different the experiences of foremothers had been. Students compared notes on great-aunts who remained unmarried and had affairs with married men, and on grandmothers who had accepted their husbands' adultery for years. This introduced an opportunity to discuss the history of sexuality, and the changes in

---

[121] For an analysis of the various subtexts and (homo)sexuality, see Geertje Mak, *Mannelijke vrouwen: over grenzen van sekse in de negentiende eeuw*, (Manly Woman: On the Borders of Sex in the Nineteenth Century), (Amsterdam, 1997).
[122] Elsbeth Locher-Scholten, *Women and the Colonial State* (Amsterdam, 2000); and Frances Gouda, *Dutch Culture Overseas* (Amsterdam, 1995).

norms for female behaviour, a theme that was also discussed in the context of novels (*Jane Eyre*, *A hora de estrela*).

One of the striking aspects of the way the assignment worked out was that the authors looked at aspects of the foremother's life that could be interpreted as signs of emancipation. This made it possible to discuss in class the relation between women's history and the history of the women's movement. In this context, the academic debates about the concept of 'women's culture', as introduced by the American scholar Carol Smith-Rosenberg, proved very helpful.[123] The focus on cultural traditions broadened the scope of thinking about women's lives beyond the narratives of either heroic resistance or tragic victimhood.

Students learned that women's history could be more than finding out whether foremothers were feminists, that women's experiences in the private sphere might be a meaningful place where history took place. This helped them to reflect critically on history as a discipline that traditionally has described the public domain, while personal memories of private experiences were supposed to belong to the realm of family histories and/or literary representation. Thus, the distinction between public and private came to life in the classroom and was discussed from different angles.

Books, Archives, Memories
The distinction between public and private ways of recording and remembering returned explicitly in the detailed questions of Part 2 of the assignments, in which students had to look for published information about their foremother. The visit to the Information centre and Archive for the Women's Movement (founded in 1935) was crucial to this aspect of the assignment. Students learned about the long tradition of women taking care to preserve their history. The IIAV has an interesting policy of collecting material: archives of women's organisations and feminists, but also personal documents from women who have never played a role in public life, but who documented their lives in letters and diaries. The visit included explanations about this policy, and about the way such women's institutions can exist – through the help of volunteers, through

---

[123] Ellen DuBois, Mari Jo Buhle, Temma Kaplan, Gerda Lerner and Carroll Smith-Rosenberg, "Politics and Culture in Women's History: A Symposium." *Feminist Studies* 6. 1 (1980), 26-49.

governmental support, and through private sponsors, was an important element in the class.

The students learned that information available about women's experiences takes very disparate forms. Only part of the information could be found in history books, and in archival collections that contain primary sources, like diaries and letters. This information was mostly general, about a certain class, about a specific period, or about a certain type of work; for example, the scholarly research about the lives of servant girls was often used. This information had to be matched with knowledge that was handed down in 'the family way': memories of children and nieces, told by the biographers' mothers, fathers or aunts. Apart from this, there were other aspects of private life that have been recorded mainly in fiction. Ever the schoolmarm, I taught my students that novels should never be used indiscriminately as a historical source.

Yet, it is a fact that novels describe many joys and dilemmas in a woman's life that remain unrecorded in other forms of history and memory: whether the misery of unwanted pregnancy, the pleasures of a beautiful piece of needlework, or the dilemmas facing a girl when she wants to get married. As Nancy Armstrong put it, women's history is written in fiction.[124] To students, the challenge lay in arranging such incompatible sources of knowledge and the dissimilar viewpoints from which memories had been recorded into one presentation or story. How should knowledge stored in academic and national history books be combined with the memories of a jealous sister, for example? Would they use women's personal stories to correct academic studies about the Second World War, or would they use history books to put personal accounts and family histories into perspective?

History, Literary Criticism and Interdisciplinary Women's Studies
For this part of the assignment, it proved very useful that students read and discussed, not only scholarly texts in the class, but novels also. The assignment explicitly let students choose their own format and genre. Experimenting with form often proved useful to solve problems of disparate types of information: students used a first,

---

[124] Nancy Armstrong, "Literature as Women's History." *Genre XIX* (Winter 1986), 347-369.

second or third person narrative, or a combination of these. Sometimes they included footnotes and used these to reflect on the way they had obtained their information. Some opted for a story illustrated with photographs, others told it as a hypertext with different parts. Through working on this assignment, students came to realise that novels contain types of narrative that do more justice to the lives of their foremothers than a political or economic history of their fatherland ever could. The complex de-centred prose of the modernist author Djuna Barnes might serve better to describe women's position within a patrilineal genealogy than an overview of the struggle for suffrage. Toni Morrison's complex narrative in *Beloved* is probably more effective in portraying the experience of slavery and the struggle to become a subject than a cliometric analysis of the economic profitability of slavery.

One of the most rewarding aspects of the assignment, in the context of this class, was that the idea of a non-hierarchical interdisciplinary practice of historical and literary studies to understand women's lives became palpable and do-able for the students. For this assignment, the students drew on expert knowledge from various disciplines of the Humanities and experimented with ways of integrating this into a life story that captured the life of a foremother. They understood that the problematic of women's role in history is not only about the collection of facts about their lives, but also about the politics of memory. They learned that national histories that describe the developments in the public domain do not lend themselves to tell the stories of private experiences. The gendered opposition between history and literary fiction was deconstructed by the students themselves.[125] The assignment helped them to see women's history as part of the interdisciplinary Women's Studies.

Bibliography
Ellen DuBois, Mari Jo Buhle, Temma Kaplan, Gerda Lerner and Carroll Smith-Rosenberg. "Politics and Culture in Women's History: A Symposium" in *Feminist Studies*. 6. 1. (1980): 26-49.
In this document, scholars in American women's history discuss the way women's cultural traditions, formed in the private sphere of

---

[125] *ibid.*

family life, are related to the struggle for women's liberation. The work of Caroll Smith-Rosenberg about the 'women's world of love and rituals' in white middle class US in the nineteenth century is discussed. For Women's Studies students, the lively debate of short and sharp contributions is a good introduction to the problem of how to interpret private women's experiences in the domestic sphere. Students may also read "The Female World of Love and Ritual: Relations between Women in Nineteenth-Century America" by Smith-Rosenberg, Carroll in *Signs* Vol. 1 (1975), but this debate is shorter and more accessible because it contains different opinions that may inspire students.

Nancy Armstrong. "Literature as Women's History" in *Genre XIX*. (Winter 1986): 347-369.

This introduction to a special issue of a literary genre contains a short, but very insightful, summary of the thesis that the distinction between history and literary criticism is a gendered opposition, and that Women's Studies scholars should take serious literary texts as sources for women's history. Armstrong argues (as she does in her book *Desire and Domestic Fiction: A Political History of the Novel* (Oxford UP, 1987), that novels of the eighteenth and early nineteenth centuries, document the rise of the gendered private sphere where women were responsible for moral and sexual education. For students who write about the private life of their foremothers and have to combine information from history books with information from domestic sources, this historisisation of the private sphere is very useful. It will also help students to take novels serious as contributing to gendered identities.

Bonnie Smith. "On Writing Women's Work" in *EUI Working Paper*. HEC No. 91/71.

This is an interesting, but not very well known paper, by Bonnie Smith. She describes and analyses the way in which women social scientists and political activists in the early decades of the twentieth century began to write the lives of working class women. Smith then continues on to the contributions of working class women themselves to this genre of social reporting. The article is very helpful because it addresses not only the contents of those life stories, but also the style.

It shows how different literary forms do different things with life stories. Students faced with the challenge to create a text themselves can profit from this – it makes them aware of the pitfalls of scientific writing about women as objects of social research.

Carolyn Heilbrun. *Writing a Woman's Life.* **New York, 1988.**
This is a very helpful and insightful text about the differences between biographies of men and women. It addresses the difficulty of writing a woman's life when her experiences do not fit the 'male model' of *bildung* and a public career. Students writing about their foremothers felt especially inspired by the idea that the later (middle-age) part of a woman's life may be as interesting as the first decades.

Alice Walker. *In Search of Our Mother's Gardens: Womanist Prose.* **The Women's Press, 1984.**
Several articles in this collection were very useful in this class. Alice Walker addresses the problem of writing about herself as an author when no examples of biographies and historical writing are available to reflect her experiences. Her argument that the quest for beauty that she finds in her mother's love for creating a garden helps her to understand her own artistic aspirations, and gives them 'a history' that is enlightening. It helped students to see cultural traditions that had been invisible because they have not become part of cultural histories.

Jolande Withuis. "De doorbraak en de feestrok. Een uitnodiging tot onderzoek naar de politieke geschiedenis van sekse rond het einde van de tweede wereldoorlog."(The breakthrough of the patchwork celebration skirt. An invitation for research about the history of gender at the end of World War II.) *De Gids.* **Vol. 154 (1991), 255-268. See also: Jolande Withuis. "Patchwork Politics in the Netherlands, 1946-50: Women, Gender and the World War II trauma." In** *Women's History Review.* **Vol. 3 (1994). 3: 293-313**.
This article provides a detailed historical description and an insightful reflection on the way private memories and public discourse mixed in the Netherlands at the end of the Second World War. The example is the organised movement of women who wanted to commemorate the war in the Netherlands via patchwork skirts that contained pieces of

fabric reminding women of their experiences. The text offers great insight into the way private and public were (re-)defined after the war, and the forms of women's exclusion from the public sphere of politics in the Netherlands.

Mineke Bosch. *Politics and Friendship: Letters from the International Woman Suffrage Alliance, 1902-1942.* **Columbus: Ohio State UP, 1990.**
Mineke Bosch analyses the letters exchanged by suffragists around the Dutch Aletta Jacobs, and uses this material for an insightful reflection on the way private relations and politics mixed in the women's movement. The book uses many letters that are kept in the International Information Centre and Archive of the Women's Movement in Amsterdam (IIAV). For the collections of both private and public papers from women, see www.iiav.nl (website also available in English).

Maria Grever. *Strijd tegen de stilte : Johanna Naber (1859-1941) en de vrouwenstem in geschiedenis.* **(Struggle Against the Silence. Johanna Naber (1859-1941) and the Women's Voice in History) Hilversum: Verloren, 1994.**
This dissertation is about a Dutch woman who wrote history books both about Dutch national history and about the history of Dutch women and the women's movement. Grever describes both the way Naber was excluded from academic education and from academic discussion, and the ways in which Naber dealt with this marginalisation in her work. For an exploration of the way historical novels offered women an opportunity to write history see: Maria Grever, et al. eds. *Gender en genre van de historische roman. Tijdschrift voor geschiedenis.* (Gender and Genre of the Historical Novel. Special Issue of *Dutch Journal for History*) Groningen: Wolters-Noordhoff, 1999.

Women's Account of their Memories of War
María Suárez Lafuente

Illustration: Book cover: a militia woman holding a child in Dulce Chacón, La voz dormida. Madrid, Alfaguara, 2002.

The Context

This seminar was offered within the Doctoral Programme on Women's Studies at the University of Oviedo, Spain. The programme is interdisciplinary and receives students from any field of study, but mostly from philology, history, law, sociology, psychology and medicine; most of the students (never more than 25) are women in their twenties and come from the Principality of Asturias, where the university is grounded, one-fourth of them usually come from other places in Spain, and a mere ten per cent come from South America.

The programme on Women's Studies offers an ample basis in feminist methodologies and feminist knowledge, which includes the analysis and practice of feminist discourses. There is a section devoted to the recovery of women's names and actions, which is where this seminar was introduced, as a sort of 'archaeology of knowledge'. Then there is a final round-up where we look at the different academic disciplines with such an integral point of view as possible.

The programme covers thirty-two credits, twelve credits corresponding to an M.A. Thesis, which each student must write during the second year. The first year of the programme is devoted to the remaining twenty credits, each of which entails ten hours of teaching. Methodological and introductory courses take up fifty hours, while seminars on different aspects of women's activities take up to thirty hours. "Women's Accounts of their Memories of War" covers three credits, divided into ten three-hour sessions, during a trimester. The seminar is conducted throughout by only one lecturer.

Course Description

Students get the syllabus of the seminar when they register for the programme either in July or September – that is at least six or four months before the seminar takes place, which allows them enough time to read the compulsory list and think about the proposed topics. The reading list is ample, but very simple pertaining to discourse, structure or academic analysis; furthermore, the topics are familiar to the students, the Spanish War being often in the news and still a topic of conversation in family gatherings. The course is divided into five sections, each one consisting of two sessions of three hours. The sections cover the following topics:

- o   Women's invisibility in official war accounts
- o   Official spaces
- o   Public / private spaces
- o   Enclosed / private spaces
- o   The experience of war

The first and last sections consist of in-class discussions about the circumstances and possibilities posed by history as it has been written (section 1) and history as it should stand (section 5). Students should find examples in the bibliography for the other three sections. This helps the class to discuss the spaces women are allowed to inhabit, while throwing light on women's approaches to misfortune, their adaptation to given circumstances, and their capacity for survival. Since several of the books (those by Suárez Coalla, Cueva Fernández and Castañón and Koska's documentary) consist of compilations of women's remembrances, students are asked to record a short interview with a woman of their circle. The interview need only be the registering of some specific memory, but within the topics discussed during the seminar, and must respond to some of the problematic aspects that had been pointed out during classes.

Reflection and Evaluation
Official spaces: War is Not a Women's Issue (?)
The aim of the seminar is the recognition of women's experience in one of the historical events that sadly marked the history of Spain in the twentieth century. Moreover, it also aims to give lived experience its due historical dimension. If experience is one-sided, so are the official historical accounts, biased by patriarchal perception, where women are obliterated without a glance backwards. It is no less important that recording experience activates dark, suppressed memories, also part of the development of people and events. As Mary Clancy writes in her paper, introducing women's narratives of experience shows the contrasts and diversity in history and opens up a new intellectual and political space.

This space is not only new, with all that 'newness' entails: another, always enriching, point of view, a point of contrast, the confirmation and amplification of given data and the rehabilitation of suppressed lives; this new space is also an educational space where women can organise their memories, articulate their thoughts, learn the value of their experience, see it as a communal effort for the benefit of all, gain in self-esteem, appreciate their political value in a historical context, find a language of their own and redefine their own private space as something of general importance.

After this reflection, we start the research project by stating a couple of obvious facts: that women undoubtedly form at least half of the population, and, at times of war, the percentage of women escalates steadily every day, as men are killed in battle, in guerrilla warfare, or by disease and infections. Also, regardless of the number of books we consult about war or the number of movies about war we see, women amount to practically nothing, they are never protagonists, not even secondary characters, they are merely props and always fill the same roles: nurses, lovers or mothers. But the fact remains that women are not only present in any war, they also fight for their ideals, they are involved in the fate of different factions, they suffer the consequences of war, and they are used and abused.

In Hugh Thomas's history, *The Spanish Civil War* (1961) – one of the first books to be written to explain the conflagration – out of some 2300 index entries (833.911 in the 1971 Penguin edition) only 51 are women: approximately 2.2 % of the total. But of those 51 entries, 27 are foreign women, mentioned once because they favoured one faction or another. Out of the remaining 24, 15 are subsidiary figures, as wives or pre-war activists. So, in fact, only 9 (0.3 %) are women that merit a mention through their connection with the war. Thus, the question is: why is it that women are omitted in accounts of war? "There are so many men who know exactly how things happened, why don't they write about it? Why?" (Yina Castañón 122). Petö and Waaldijk offer an answer: those who win a war do not want to hear any other version but their own, and, therefore, keep history "narrowed down to an enforced forgetting" because "private knowledge and private histories [will] challenge official representations".[126] The class reacts with ire to these words: they want to challenge every historical page, they want to inscribe women's voices everywhere, and they want to make women visible. But equally important is the fact that they now understand the meaning of de Beauvoir's words, "the personal is political".

The books that are listed in the bibliography have mostly been published only in the last few years, as in Spain there had been an agreed silence about the personal experiences of war, so as not to interfere with the shaky democratic transition that started in 1975. These books are compilations of personal accounts, given by women, of how they experienced the war, or fictional renderings of family memories. We decided to put both, the fictional and the 'real', on the same level, then we could state that all of them proceed from

---

[126] Andrea Petö and Berteke Waaldijk, "Writing the Lives of Foremothers, the History and Future of a Feminist Teaching Tool" in *The Making of European Women's Studies*, Athena Vol. IV. (Utrecht, 2002), 150.

experiences that have a lot in common, and some even mention the same events; the fictional accounts simply provide an ampler context for the war memories. The informants in these books were born within the first twenty years of the twentieth century. With very few exceptions – be they urban or rural, republican or nationalist – what they now remember is not the political motivation, but the day-to-day of war: finding food, hiding, nursing, connecting parties and passing information.

Public/Private Spaces

One common feature in all the accounts is the fact that the war ended any pretence of privacy. The war permeated every corner of life; every space was public, liable to be invaded, registered, open to anybody's gaze. Thus, without having a say in the process, women were tossed into the space always forbidden to them. Their traditional roles were transformed, or dissolved, at convenience.

The change was so radical and sudden that one of the most important facts in all these post-war memories is that, during the war, women had to step into the public sphere: they came out of the house to work in armament factories and in the textile war industry, to clean up after bombardments, to help in farms and in hospitals. This experience is remembered with satisfaction. Informants still feel the elation of 'being useful', of 'working'. (At this point there were sub-discussions about the low social consideration of housework, which does not even amount to 'work', and about the ensuing low self-esteem of housewives and their sense of dependence' even in contemporary life). Their success 'outside the house' enhances their self-esteem and makes them, in looking backwards, feel proud of themselves.

The anecdote recalled by writer Dolores Medio about two of her aunts, aged 70 and 90, was chosen by the class as the best example of how war could also be remembered positively by women, since they felt a whiff of independence. Medio's aunts, left alone in the besieged Oviedo, managed, all by themselves and in spite of their "frailty and infirmity", to get a pass from the military authorities, to cross the frontline and to travel a hundred kilometres of occupied land to find their niece, who was at the time teaching in a remote village in the Asturian mountains. Medio summarises how one of them, Auntie

Lola, "had always lived with us, not only as an economically dependent member, but also installed in that spiritual dependence expected from a spinster in the family. She now enjoyed this new life as a jubilant renaissance" (180-81). Nevertheless, and in spite of the joy of independence in some of the accounts, the sense of desolation and fear is not to be minimised. Desolation and fear were felt, mainly, in closed spaces: when in hiding, in shelters during bombardments, or, worst of all, in prison.

Enclosed/Private Spaces

Women adapted well to the new circumstances in the forced transition that left their lives in the open. They adapted equally well to the enforced enclosure of prisons. María Salvo, in Koska's documentary, is certain that women in prison survived their ordeal because they organised themselves. They organised schools to teach the illiterate, workshops to sew clothes for themselves and to make some money, they created a structure to support each other, to nurse the sick, to back the desperate. They even organised parties and celebrated festivities. Yina Castañón gives extensive information on how women were involved, from the prison cell, in the education of their children, left alone to fend for themselves in the streets. They gave them, during their fortnightly visit, not only moral advice, but also practical tips to keep life in order until their mothers came out.

Women in prisons constitute a large part of these war memories for several reasons, not least that many of them had fought openly in the Republican army, which provided them with an articulate political discourse that helped them to explain their position. Also, they are known within the inner history of political parties and are easier to locate. There were women imprisoned simply because they were related to 'enemies' of the Regime, or because their men were in flight. Many of these were illiterate, but found a way of expressing themselves through close contact with the political prisoners.

Suárez Coalla's book deals mainly with the experience of women left at home without men, and who had to rise to the solution of needs that had, hitherto, been the domain of the men of the house, such as working the fields to get some food for the family and some fodder for the cattle that remained, as well as cope with cattle raising, caring for the children, the old and the infirm, mending the house, hiding from soldiers and bombings, and finding hiding spaces for their own or passing men fleeing from the enemy. The accounts contained in Coalla's book were closer to those heard at home by the students in the class, and were welcomed with the spirit of recognition. Thus, students were able to contribute with stories heard, stories lived by their own female relatives; they felt the need to put them down on paper and, once more, realised the joy of feeling that private experience is also what history is made of.

Evaluation

By the end of the ten weeks, we can list several guidelines that provide no conclusion to the theme of the course, but can help structure future research to be conducted individually or in several other seminars:

o   Women are part of the war experience.
o   Therefore, war history is flawed if the female experience is not taken into account.
o   Women rise up to any condition, however desperate or glorious it might be.
o   Women are not 'sweet little things', but persons, luckily varied and complex.
o   Post-war life would have been impracticable if women had not been active in the rearguard during the conflict, keeping up business, land, cattle, factories and family life.

'Women and their lives during the Spanish Civil War' is a life-long project, but it is also very rewarding, in the short term as this thirty-hour seminar shows. It touches upon political/feminist issues at large, as women's activities do not only extend to archetypically male territories, but are proficiently executed. Therefore, the gendering of history proves to be an unquestionable need; if it has to be done through a history of life-events, this is only due to the resistance offered by male history throughout and not because the still 'female side of history' is less important or interesting.

The sum of the experiences told in the books of this bibliography, with the stories the students brought to class, amounts to an active, positive, hard account of contemporary Spanish history, a history that looks forwards to a better future for all. This could explain why patriarchy is so intent on keeping women imprisoned in the weak end of dichotomies, maybe patriarchy is scared of seeing its reflection in the human mirror.

Suggested Reading

Ángeles Caso. *Un largo silencio.* (A long silence) Barcelona: Planeta, 2000.

Yina Castañón. *Realidad, vivencias e historia.* (Reality, experience and history) Principado de Asturias, Asturias, 1991.

Dulce Chacón. *La voz dormida.* (The sleeping voice) Madrid: Alfaguara, 2002.

Isabel Cueva Fernández. *¡La retaguardia nos pertenece! Las mujeres de izquierdas en Asturias (1936-1937).* (The rearguard is ours! Leftist women in Asturias 1936-37) Ayuntamiento de Gijón, 2000.

Susana Koska. (Director) *Mujeres en pie de Guerra.* (Women in Arms) A Documentary. Barcelona, 2004.

Dolores Medio. *Atrapados en la ratonera. El sitio de Oviedo.* (Caught in the Mouse-trap. The Siege of Oviedo) Madrid: Ediciones Alce, 1980.

Mary Nash. *Rojas.* (Red) Madrid: Taurus, 1999.

Andrea Pető and Berteke Waaldijk. "Writing the Lives of Foremothers, the History and Future of a Feminist Teaching Tool" in *The Making of European Women's Studies.* Athena Vol. IV. Universiteit Utrecht, 2002, 149-161.

Paquita Suárez Coalla. La mió vida ye una novela. (My life is a Novel) Oviedo, Trabe, 2001.

Hugh Thomas. *The Spanish Civil War.* Hammondsworth, Penguin Books, 1971

Bibliography

Dulce Chacón. *La voz dormida, Alfaguarra.* (The Sleeping Voice) Madrid, 2002

This is a fictionalised story based on oral accounts about the day-to-day life of some women in Cárcel de Ventas, Madrid, in the years following the Spanish War. Some of them had been active against the Francoist troops, one way or another, actually fighting, loading ammunition, carrying messages or food, or hiding people. Some others simply happened to be the daughters or sisters of known Republicans. Regardless of the political 'sin' committed, they strove to survive in such close, impossible spaces as the Ventas Prison. They were not impervious to political tensions and everyday misgivings, but they found a way to fight off humiliation and tortures, and helped one another to overcome the fear of impending death.

Chacón registers some unofficially known episodes from the war. A significant one is the frustrated embarkation of Republican people in the port of Valencia at the end of the war by several allied ships that never showed up, thus causing the death and imprisonment of thousands of people, since Franco's troops did keep the appointment. This book also fictionalises the impact of the execution of the Twelve Roses: twelve young Republican women killed at the end of the war, who became an icon of resistance for women. The novel also includes a death sentence signed at the beginning of the war against a woman accused of "procuring food for the rebels" in the orchards of Cordoba. It is a homage to Spanish women, who fought and endured the Spanish War in the same measure as men, but had always been denied a historical place in it. The invisibility of women in history is doubled, in this case, by the fact that they were on the side that lost the war.

The Principality of Asturias ed. *Realidad, vivencia e historia en la voz de Yina Castañón.* **(Life, Experience and History, in the Voice of Yina Castañón). Spain: Asturias, 1991.**

This is the biography of Yina Castañón, born in 1907 and still alive in 1991, when the book was published. Yina was a member of the Communist Party during the Second Republic, and worked as a nurse for the Republican side during the Spanish War. Imprisoned at the end of the war in Ventas, Madrid, she narrates the collective story of the women there.

Ventas was a Women's Prison projected by Victoria Kent to house two people per room. During the time of Castañón's internment, there were twenty one women per cell, and some ten thousand women in all. She describes the social structure of the building; a corridor for those active in the everyday running of the place – nurses like herself, teachers, indoors mailwomen, waitresses and so on. Prisoners in a different corridor were regarded as political, in most cases, because their male relatives had been involved on the wrong side. Another corridor was for older women, and a last one for women caught in the midst of the food black market, an imperious necessity at the time, both to eat and to survive.

Yina voices the incredulity of women faced with the fact that both the men outside and the world at large were not doing anything against Franco's regime. The men that fought or suffered the atrocities of war and were now walking freely in the streets outside should be shouting the truth and getting help from abroad to overturn such a corrupt government. Castañón praises the atmosphere of solidarity that existed in the prison, but cannot forget the feeling of fear and helplessness that pervaded everything. She was released after eight years by the mercy of Our Lady of Las Mercedes, a practice still common in Spain today when a prisoner is liberated in the festivity of either one of the local Madonnas or during the Easter week. Yina exiled herself in Venezuela and came back to live in Asturias, Spain, when democracy was established.

Fernanda Romeu Alfaro. *El silencio roto. Mujeres contra el franquismo.* **(Silence Broken. Women Against Franquism). Madrid: El Viejo Topo, 2002.**
The title alludes to the "pact of silence" agreed upon in Spain by the major political forces after Franco died in 1975 and democracy was re-established. It was feared that the wounds from the Civil War were too fresh and that speaking freely after so many years of dictatorship might be dangerous for the democratisation of the country. But Romeu Alfaro argues that it is time to break that silence, or the experiences and dramas of the war will be buried with the people that suffered them.

Alfaro analysed 899 documents written by and about women, in which their experiences during the war, the post-war times and up to 1975 were registered, in letters, diaries, notes, newspaper clips and official minutes. She then organised those memories in chronological and thematic units, and marked four temporal sections: 1939-1952, from the end of the conflict to the end of the guerrilla warfare; 1952 to 1960, a time span that saw the first women's mobilisations in peace time; 1960 to 1970, mark the first strikes after the war and the founding of the Democratic Women's Movement; and, finally, 1970 to

1975, when women vindicated their specific rights as women. In order to give some coherence to her extensive research, the author found interlocutors among those women that have been prisoners in the sadly infamous Prison of Ventas, in Madrid. The outcome is an impressive first-person, polyphonic narrative, made out of personal accounts and official dictates, through which we learn about everyday hardships – births and deaths, ambushes, firing squads, hunger, cold, pain, solitude, anger, and fear. However, we also learn about the beginnings of hope, the recovery of silenced names and the new strength to resume fighting and demonstrating.

The book recovers for history a large amount of documents that would have been otherwise lost. The author exhibits a hundred pages of authentic material, including photographed and written documentation; she also draws maps and diagrams to make the damage more obvious in ciphers and graphics, and shows that, with most men dead, missing, wounded, exiled or in hiding, Spain was mostly, and for many years, a country of women commanding the old, the infirm and the children, in spite of which, the governmental propaganda is directed throughout those times to 'manly men' and 'happy wives'.

Carlos Fonseca. *Trece rosas rojas.* (Thirteen Red Roses) [2004] Barcelona: RBA, 2005.

This is the life story of thirteen young women from Madrid, seven of them under-age, who were killed, together with forty-three others, in front of a firing squad in the summer of 1939, for no other reason than that belonged to socialist youth organisations before the war. The episode was silenced during the dictatorship, but survived through word of mouth, making the 'thirteen red roses' a symbol of women's resistance against the Franco regime.

This is the first book that has collected the biographies of these women, and it was written with the aid of oral testimonies of relatives and friends, letters written by the roses themselves while in prison, and family photographs. Fonseca also uses materials from the press archives, and from military and penitentiary archives. The main source is the set of documents concerning the judicial case against the women, with their declarations and the evidence against them, usually reported by the prosecutor, without giving exact details of its origin.

159

The book is divided into three parts: Fight, Repression and Revenge, which sum up very aptly the process of war and post-war in Spain. The author uses the development of the story to narrate some of the most important political events at the time, and also to point out the significant contribution of women to the war effort. The analysis, however, is not gender-orientated, and many opportunities are missed to explain both the danger of what women were doing and why their male contemporaries did not give them their due recognition.

Carmen Domingo. *Con voz y voto. Las mujeres y la política en España. 1931-1945.* **[With Voice and Vote. Women and Politics in Spain. 1931-1945] Barcelona: Lumen, 2004.**
This book traces the long historical path Spanish women took from 1931, when the Second Republic gave them the vote, through to the Civil War, post-war repression and autarchy. A considerable number of women were subjected to the dictates of patriarchal society through husbands and the church, but many others had a mind of their own and were active socially and politically and helped to create a plurality of political options and to further education and provide welfare for the benefit of the country.

Domingo remembers the names and lives of many women such as Federica Montseny, Victoria Kent, Clara Campoamor, Margarita Nelken, Mª Teresa León and María Lejárraga, to name but a few, all of whom excelled either in the political or cultural arena. But, parallel to these major names, the author also remembers the life and situation of women more generally at the time. The book has a set of biographies, an index of first names, and a useful bibliography. It is an excellent introduction to herstory in Spain, since it moves constantly between the general and the specific.

5.   *Writing Our Foremothers*
      Leena Kurvet-Käosaar and Redi Koobak

Illustration: Book cover: Tiina Kirss, et al., eds She Who Remembers,
Survives (Tartu University Press, 2004)

Description of the Course: 'Truth and Fiction in Autobiography'
(http://www.hot.ee/kurvet/autobiograafia.htm). Department of
Comparative Literature, Tartu University, Fall 2004. Students:
advanced BA and MA students of the Humanities.

The course provided an overview of the development of classical
autobiography theories during the last twenty years, focusing on
memory, subjectivity, representation, and the factuality and
fictionality of life-writing texts. In the seminars, the so-called canonical
autobiographies, (Augustine, Goethe), as well as the autobiographies
of well-known Estonian authors (August Kitzberg, Jaan Kross, Aino
Kallas, Käbi Laretei) were discussed. Separate sections of the course

were dedicated to women's autobiography and (non-fictional) life-writing (*Estonian Life Stories*) culminating in the foremother assignment. The foremother theme was covered over four seminars.

The Foremother Assignment

The students were asked to write either an autobiographical narrative that focuses on the foremother theme or an analysis of the foremother theme in various collections of Estonian life stories. The autobiographical narrative could focus on the students' own foremothers, but also on the concept of foremother in general and its importance in an Estonian cultural context (though still maintaining an autobiographical angle). For the analysis, the students could choose two (or more) personal narratives either from published life story collections, such as the three volumes of *Estonian Life-stories*, or find an archival source and write a comparative analysis of how the foremother theme was developed. The autobiographical narratives or analyses were distributed among all members of the class and discussed in the seminar. The students were expected to consider critically the key issues of life-writing theories covered by lectures – lecture notes were available on the course homepage – and raised in required readings that included selected chapters of *Reading Autobiography: A Guide for Interpreting Life Narratives*[127] and a number of articles on women's autobiography (for example, Susan Stanford Friedman's "Women's Autobiographical Selves" (1988) and Doris Sommer's "Not Just a Personal Story: Women's Testimonies and the Plural Self" (1988).[128]

---

[127] Sidonie Smith and Julia Watson, *Reading Autobiography: A Guide for Interpreting Life Narratives*, (U of Minnesota Press, 2002).

[128] In addition, the following sources were available to students: Rutt Hinrikus, (ed.), *Estonian Life-Stories*, Vol. I-III. (Tallinn: Tänapäev, 2000-2003); Pető and Waaldijk, "Writing the Lives of Foremothers, the History and Future of a Feminist Teaching Tool," in Rosi Braidotti *et al*, (eds.), *The Making of European Women's Studies*, Vol. IV ATHENA, (Utrecht, 2002), 149-161; Tiina Kirss, Ene Kõresaar and Marju Lauistin, (eds.), *She Who Remembers, Survives*, (Tartu UP, 2004); Redi Koobak, "Genderedness of Memory: Reconceptualizing Herstories," (Presentation in class, available also in *Ariadne Lõng* 2005), 188-191; Conference 'Face to Face with our Foremothers' (*Esiemaga silmitsi*), organised by Estonian Women Students' Society (ENÜS. Leena Kurvet-Käosaar is a member of the organisation and was one of the conference organisers) and Domus Dorpatensis, (Nov. 2004). Students of the course were invited to participate in the conference; Aija Sakova, 'Knowing Our Foremothers Helps to Learn about Society' (Interview with Leena Kurvet-Käosaar and Redi Koobak), in *Universitas Tartuensis*, (Dec 17, 2004), 3.

Importance of the Foremother Assignment as a Teaching Practice

The set-up of the assignment, requiring the students to include personal reflection and inviting them to re-evaluate and deconstruct the concept of history from a gendered perspective, differed from a traditional study task in the Estonian academic context. As the interconnectedness and/or split between the private and public sphere is an important focus of feminist thought in general, I hoped to draw the students' attention to it via a practical and rarely used type of study task. The assignment also required the students to include a personal perception of time and history and, via this, to notice and learn to evaluate critically socio-cultural processes of the construction of history. It also encouraged the students to build a gendered identity across generations and, more generally, to address the generation issue in the processes of constructing their own identities and subjectivities.

The majority of students wrote an autobiographical narrative focusing on a female relative, grandmother or great-grandmother. One student conducted research on a woman who was the author of numerous history textbooks and a political activist. From the 1920s, another contribution focused on her older brother as a foremother figure. In addition, Redi Koobak, who has taken Andrea Pető's foremother class at Central European University, participated in the seminars. She gave an overview of her work on Leida Laius, one of the very few Estonian film directors, but she also composed an autobiographical narrative of her grandmother and analysed the differences between the two types of assignments.

The student essays and class discussion indicated that the assignment was taken very seriously and a lot of time and effort was dedicated to completing it. A number of students pointed out during the discussion that the assignment crossed the boundaries of a typical course assignment and became an important occasion for rethinking one's identity and relation to history from a gendered perspective. Most narratives were deeply personal, raising issues of loss, painful adaptations, the limits of woman's lifespan in its specific socio-cultural environment and strategies of overcoming them, patterns of care and deprivation. As the students knew beforehand that the narratives were going to be distributed among the course participants, the choice of the perspective reflected willingness and need to bring up personal issues in a class context.

The discussion showed that students appreciated the personal angle of each other's stories and displayed subtle and considerate discussion skills, so that little moderation by me, as instructor, was needed. A more difficult part of the discussion was the process of placing the individual narratives into a wider context, relating them to the concepts of history and autobiography, and problematising these concepts via the narratives. Initially, the students were somewhat hesitant to submit their narratives to critical analysis in terms of narrative structure, imagery, and the process of textual construction of a foremother, and to accept the discussion results as knowledge.

The fact that personal narratives have become a canonised genre in Estonian culture, via the publication of three extensive volumes of Estonian life stories, certainly helped the students to relate their own narratives to the larger cultural contexts. I, as instructor, also tried to minimise my facilitation of the discussion and emphasised the collective learning experience during the seminars. In order to accomplish this better, I participated in the assignment myself, presenting a narrative of my maternal grandmother as my foremother. In addition, I documented the course of the discussion carefully and published it on the course homepage, emphasising its status as collectively gained new knowledge created in the class.[129] I also had a rare opportunity to make use of the expertise and experience of the foremother topic of Redi Koobak, a doctoral student at Tartu University. Redi's thoughts on the assignment are included below.

A View from Multiple Positions
Redi Koobak
My initial contact with the concept of 'foremother' in Andrea Pető's course 'Historical Frames of Identity and Locating Women's Memories in History' at CEU, Hungary in Spring 2004, was rather illuminating. As a student of Gender Studies, I was aware of how gender, race and class intersect to construct individual lives and constitute major social inequalities between different groups in society. However, it was not until I began reflecting more deeply on

---

[129] http://www.hot.ee/kurvet/konspektid/AB/esiema_kokkuvote.htm

the politics of gendered remembering for the foremother assignment, which was part of the course, that I realised how challenging, yet extremely important, it is to re-conceptualise history in order to make sense of the present.

Presenting my work on Leida Laius, an important and admired Estonian film director, who I had chosen as my foremother for Andrea Pető's class, at a conference, 'Face to Face with our Foremothers' in Tartu, Estonia in November 2004, as well as in Leena Kurvet-Käosaar's course, 'Truth and Fiction in Autobiography', also in 2004, gave me a new impulse to reconsider my thoughts on the matter and encouraged me to further contemplate on the concept of 'foremother'.[130] Inspired by the personal foremother stories of Kurvet-Käosaar's students, I shared my grandmother, Leida Kuldpere's, story with the class where I was not really participating as a student who has taken on an 'obligation' to do the class assignments by signing up for the course at the beginning of the semester, but, rather, as an outsider with previous 'expert' knowledge and experience on the subject. Bringing in a very personal paradigm to the discussion of foremothers in which I had previously engaged in from a 'safe' distance and a somewhat uncommitted position, not really going further from a theoretical level, put everything into a new perspective.

What emerged as the most significant lesson for me from the discussions with Leena Kurvet-Käosaar and her class was the realisation that while the personal dimension is unquestionably essential in making sense of the wider framework, we need to constantly ask critical questions about the way we construct and structure stories. We must keep in mind who tells what stories to whom, considering carefully what the questions are that need to be asked. In other words, it is important to be just as critical of the narrative structures we use when telling personal stories as we are of traditional historical narratives. In the course of reconstructing my grandmother's story from my own memories, as well as those of my relatives, I realised how easy it is to fall into the trap of becoming overtly sentimental and presenting an idealised image of a foremother that is no different from the same traditional narrative framework that I had been so critical of. I became aware of the (his)story writer's

---

[130] http://www.hot.ee/kurvet/konspektid/AB/esiema_Redi.htm

enormous power and responsibility – the freedom to choose what to tell and what to leave untold.

Participating in the various discussions of foremothers as a student in a classroom consisting of participants from diverse cultural backgrounds, as a presenter at a conference devoted specifically to this topic and an 'expert' outsider in an open and highly personal classroom discussion considerably widened my perspective on the topic. From the comparison of the narrative structures of my stories of the two Leida's, it became evident how both narratives re-conceptualised the relationship between the individual and the society in constructing and reconstructing gender roles, female subjectivity, and its perception by others. In order to understand the different perspectives that structure the ways in which we write about women and how we remember them, we need to analyse all the different roles and ways in which women have traditionally been portrayed in history.

Main Clusters of Issues Emerging from the Discussions

The Concept of the Foremother

- o Moving toward a concept via personal experience
- o Overlapping and contrasting foremother models in the narratives
- o Different ways of structuring the narratives (chronological, episodic, fragmented) and their effect on the concept of the foremother

Sources
What counts as a source?

- o Abundance of documents around us, the importance of family documents (photographs, letters, official documents, diaries, also the absence of such documents)
- o The importance of the addressee in the cases when material is collected via informal interviews or conversations. (Who tells what stories to whom? What are the questions to be asked?)
- o The sentimental value of the material

'Scales' for positioning our foremothers

- o   Ordinary >< exceptional, Inhabiting private >< public sphere
- o   Time frames, the relationship of the past and the present (Continuity? Disruption? Other possibilities?)
- o   The role of gender, social position, and national identity.

Suggested Reading

Tiina Kirss, Ene Kõresaar and Marju Lauristin. *She Who Remembers, Survives. Interpreting Estonian Women's Post-Soviet Life Stories.* Tartu UP, 2004.

Leena Kurvet-Käosaar. "Imagining a Hospitable Community in the Deportation and Emigration Narratives of Baltic Women." *Prose Studies: History, Theory, Criticism.* Vol. 26, No 1-2: 59–78.

Leena Kurvet-Käosaar. "'Other Things Happened to Women:' World War II, Violence and Discourses of National Identity in *A Sound of the Past* by Käbi Laretei and *The Woman In Amber* by Agate Nesaule." *Journal of Baltic Studies.* (Fall 2003) 313-331.

Vieda Skultans. *Testimony of Lives. Narrative and Memory in Post-Soviet Latvia.* London and New York: Routledge, 1997.

Vieda Skultans. "Theorizing Latvian Lives: The Quest for Identity." *Journal of the Royal Anthropological Institute.* Vol. 3. Issue 4, (Dec. 1997): 761-780.

6. Memories, Histories and Narratives
Mary Clancy

Illustration: 'Anonymous smile: resting woman worker, west of Ireland, 1940s'. (personal archive)

Explanations, Descriptions and Scope of Study
This contribution is based on my experience of using research-based project work on courses for adults returning to university-level education.[131] It reflects on how research-based strategies ideally suit the adult learner and the historian interested in life stories. The core question of recognising experience, for instance, is common to each group. The contribution will take into account the constraints and possibilities of doing research on courses of short duration where resources of time and money are limited. Therefore, this discussion

---

[131] Mary Clancy, Caitríona Clear, Tríona Nic Giolla Choille and Alan Hayes, (eds.), "Oral History and Biography." *Women's Studies Review*, Vol. 7, (Galway, 2000). For examples of student work, see "Work in Progress," 143-158.

will focus mostly on the issues that doing research in women's history involves and will include examples of stories uncovered.

Firstly, I will elaborate on the requirement to situate experience (of teaching and research) in 'the context of European and world history'. This makes sense given the gap in comparative study. Additionally, themes identified on the basis of multiple stories will help to inform and explain local (regional) conditions. The roles of women during periods of political and revolutionary change, for instance, is an obvious example of women's public work in certain European countries during the late nineteenth and early twentieth centuries. A writing of multiple biographies, taking into account how or why women organised differently across the social classes, is one possible method of identifying women's efforts. Such an approach can then lead to an analysis of how political achievement is constructed, reported and rewarded. In recording 'memories, histories and narratives', the researcher gives status to voices and words. In doing so and in observing the diversity of such experience, the researcher is also giving status to new intellectual and political space.

Doing Research-based Project Work: Teaching Women's History on Women's Studies Courses in NUI, Galway and Outreach Centre, County Clare.

Background

When teaching history on Certificate and Diploma courses in Women's Studies, a co-tutor and I introduced project-based assessment in place of the required essay on a prescribed topic. This approach was a success, it was popular with students, and there was much learned about how to organise research in a part-time teaching context.

Women's Studies was included also on the syllabus of an evening degree programme held at an outreach centre (Ennis, County Clare). This time, I was the sole tutor on the women's history course. Final assessment was by examination, but it was possible to include a question about doing research on the examination paper. The benefit to the student remains, in effect, the same, in that she has gathered information that she would not have gathered under conventional assessment criteria. In asking students to discuss the learning gained as a result of doing research, the student is reflecting upon the process. Analytical reflection does not end at this point. Students continue to discuss the value of their work after course completion.

Practical Issues

Class size usually ranged from 12 to 15 students, and so was amenable to the time-consuming effort of such project work at this level. There was no funding for photo-copying, telephone interviewing, or visiting archives outside of the area. The research, then, had to be managed in the context of what was available locally, or at little cost. Records, like the census returns, for instance, are available only in the home county (administrative district) of the student or, centrally in the National Archives in Dublin. This is an important, and popular, source for students writing life histories. We overcame this obstacle in various ways – students tie in research on visits home, write to the archive, get someone to print out the information or communicate over the 'phone – but this is fairly typical of what any historian might expect to come across. The same conditions apply to birth, marriage and death registers – important sources in building up life histories, but available, again, only in the home county or in Dublin. The increasing use of technology will help, especially for those living at some distance from central repositories or those with no or little funding, as students returning to formal education. Electronic sources will enable researchers to consult a much greater range of source material or to prepare in advance of a visit to an archive.[132]

In addition to the usual tasks of helping a student to identify a topic, and to contextualise and locate primary sources, the tutor needs to be able to listen. There is much that is personal and sensitive. How to advise students in certain circumstances, indeed, requires care in ensuring that they get to tell the story while, at the same time, ensuring anonymity. In one instance, for instance, merely deleting the name of a town was the key to granting a student the reassurance to continue.

---

[132] The Directory of Sources for Women's History in Ireland, for instance, is an excellent recent development: references to over 14,000 collections and sources in 262 repositories throughout Ireland.

Teaching, Timing and Building Research Skills

Timing is an important consideration. It is important to have some class-work done and, if possible, an initial assessment. A critique-type assessment,[133] for instance, is an ideal step towards project work. It helps to build analytical skills and confidence. The piece may also be used to challenge or to inform. An alternative initial assessment could be the carrying out of an interview or the writing of a short biographical piece – again, useful practice for later research. More generally, it is also important to encourage a critical approach to the reading of history and to ensure that there is adequate time to discuss research progress in class time.

Course Content and Using Secondary Source Material in Class

A key objective in class is to introduce the student to histories of women. It aims to broaden the knowledge base of students who did not learn about women's histories in school. The method is to combine texts, experience and ideas, and evaluation of primary source material. Assessment usually involves doing a critique of a text/source, in addition to final examination or project. The focus is mostly on Ireland. Certain subjects – like emigration, notably, but also the history of feminism – require a comparative approach. Emigration is an important question in Irish history with women ordinarily comprising about 50% of those who left; it is a subject with much scope. In the case of feminism, it is necessary to understand how the constitutional union between Ireland and England affected the development of feminism differently in each country.

The range of secondary source material, including collected essays and biographies, on the key areas – work, politics, feminism, philanthropy, religion – is generally good. Much remain to be done, however, especially in areas where women are found in significant numbers, like emigration, domestic service, farming women, or on questions like women running households (widows, single women) or women in institutions (mental health hospitals, Magdalen asylums, jails). Nonetheless, there is a good basis from which to grow. Of help too, in class, are collections like the *Irish Women's History Reader*[134] and

---

[133] Diary extracts, for example, letters or short articles written by or about women, are especially useful.

[134] Alan Hayes and Diane Urquhart, (eds.), *Irish Women's History Reader*, (Routledge, 2000).

the various volumes of the *Women's Studies Review*. Journal articles are as valuable to the student as to the tutor. In addition, extracts and texts are usually provided in the form of a class 'handout'.

Using Experience in Class

The following section will discuss how using primary sources in class helps to prepare the way for writing the research project. Students raise issues in class or introduce information in response to texts. Such discussion refers to personal experience or memories and is excellent preparation for doing research later. Above all, the discussion gives weight to subject matter not, or not much, treated in general histories. Students have contributed information about: why people married in the past (economic reasons and matchmaking); burying babies who are not baptised (such babies had designated burial grounds outside of church cemeteries); varieties of household and farm work done by women; living conditions in poor-quality housing; women managing families on their own; women traditional musicians; women keening (a 'crying' role for women during funerals in the past).[135] The use of video documentaries helps to extend the scope of experience, stimulate ideas and suggest new approaches. Radio is another medium to recommend to students outside of class.

Documents

The use of documents is an important part of the teaching schedule. This approach introduces students to the raw material of history in a way that stimulates and motivates as well as helps students to understand how history is made. Some documents used to date include diary extracts and census manuscript returns.[136] The diary extract facilitates discussion about literacy, perspective, bias and audience, for instance. The census offers enormous scope, enabling discussion on questions like source reliability or problems in categorising women's work. It enables the student to get an overview

---

[135] This latter was discussed during teaching in Connemara, where women did this type of crying-singing (with a brief demonstration in class).

[136] Of particular help is Maria Luddy, *Women in Ireland, 1800-1918: A Documentary Source*, (Cork, 1995). Newspapers are also exceptionally valuable – much commentary on, for instance, events such as the role of women during evictions (especially during the 1880s), working class women during elections or events like the visit of a suffragist. Advertisements – social life, work life – are also important.

of families and communities, including institutions. One student has commented on the value of getting to see the household of her local landlord.[137] Where landlord or upper-class households were elaborate, for instance, they provide excellent examples of women's work roles from governess to scullery maid. The use of documents makes discussion of literacy, language, religion and ideology more meaningful, and helps the student to develop critical, analytical skills, while also learning about life in the past.

Autobiography

In one session on autobiography, class members were invited to write a brief piece about themselves. This was introduced in class with reference to autobiographical writing and with examples taken from international as well as Irish sources. The object was to think about how we remember, how and what we select from our own past and how we write differently.

Visual Sources

The use of photographs is also popular. In class, we discuss photography, with the aid of published collections. Students can help direct discussion by bringing family photographs in to class, thus providing further basis for depictions of family life, social life or work. Artefacts also stimulate discussion and, again, students can easily bring materials in to class.[138] More generally, the pictorial depiction of the West-of-Ireland woman is an important question, given the extent to which she was idealised in photography and art (also in print). Photographic interest in another grouping, urban fishwomen (of the Claddagh village, Galway) has resulted in another good set of visual sources. Finally, photography facilitates discussion of gender and the development of this new technology in the nineteenth century, given the role of upper-class women, particularly, in amateur photography. One pioneer photographer, Augusta Clonbrock (1839-1928), lived in

---

[137] A landlord (sometimes a woman) owned the estate; the tenant rented their farm or property. Tenant-landlord relations changed significantly from the 1880s onwards, as tenant (also involving women) activities and land legislation led, eventually, to property changing hands. By c1914, the era of the old landlord class was virtually over. Religion complicated matters; in many cases, the landlord was protestant and the tenant was catholic. The West, however, had a high percentage of catholic landlords; the North had protestant tenants.
[138] I have mostly used artifacts in courses other than Women's Studies.

county Galway where her family was involved in county administration. Augusta organised women against Home Rule in the years before 1914, and was a leading philanthropist. Her work forms part of the Clonbrock Collection, now in the National Library, Dublin.

Choosing the Research Topic

The description of foremothers as 'female family-members of an earlier generation, professional predecessors or inspiring examples, political heroines', corresponds well with definitions used in class. Students have chosen mothers, grandmothers, aunts, mothers-in-law, women who were married, divorced, not married, nuns in convents, women who stayed in Ireland and women who emigrated. Some placed themselves at the centre of the narrative. Mostly, the women worked in their homes or on small farms; others worked as teachers, nurses, university lecturers, domestic servants, medical doctors or businesswomen.

Research

The value of research as a teaching tool hardly needs comment. An important point to remember, however, is that the new student sometimes finds the term itself alien, as indeed it is to anyone who does not have to 'research' as part of their daily lives.[139] To relate skills in planning, carrying out, recording and communicating research to developing personal confidence is also important. For many, there is a language or vocabulary to be learnt, a facet of doing research that also requires attention.

Choosing the Topic

Mostly, students arrive at their research idea themselves. Where the student is having difficulties, class and tutor help to suggest topics; students draw, too, on earlier reading in class. A schedule of questions helps the student to follow the conventions and to explain their idea in good detail. The student acquires skills in organising and justifying their research ideas. The tutor is more easily able to evaluate scope and access to sources.

---

[139] I came across this response in my work as research tutor in open-learning courses and have learnt to treat the concept 'research' before moving on to discuss any of its practical or methodological aspects.

For the student of women's history, the act of choosing a research topic is significant. It is, in effect, a statement that the 'ordinary' person is worthy of research, that the mother, the aunt, the grandmother is a significant historical character. The context of choosing a 'foremother' type topic is complex, however. The aim of defining new areas of significance, in line with the objectives of women's history, is potentially emancipatory for tutor and student. The realisation that someone can be studied is an opportunity to give time, thought and credit to that person in a structured fashion. It means remembering, looking for records, or interviewing people about a family member in a process that sees a certain merging of the intellectual and the emotional. Sometimes, this can be difficult – as, indeed, can any research dealing with lives led. There is enormous satisfaction, however, at family and, indeed, community level: knowledge is created or transformed; personal stories acquire historical contexts and explanations. Yet, despite the enormity of this historical achievement, the historian of women has to prove that her subject is weighty in a way that historians of political, official histories do not.

These stories of ordinary lives do regularly tell us about formal political history. This is by no means a rationale for their significance but, rather, it points to their weight as evidence. The stories are about interacting with state power at the point of experience. The stories are testimonies of living with the effects of legislation, whether relating to contraception, paid work after marriage, access to higher-grade work, equal pay, or living on a state pension.

As historians regularly attest to, interaction between the public and the private is complex. Sometimes, as in the case of social legislation, the influence of the religious is found. A sophisticated example of cross-influencing and collaboration at state-religious-judicial-family level is the experience of those children and women that court, family or priest sent to religious institutions (reformatories, industrial schools and Magdalen asylums). Supervision of research relating to such experience requires special care and, indeed, a set of clear guidelines.

Viewpoints, Examples of Research and Suggestions

Initial evaluation of the women's history courses points to students enjoying the approaches used in class. In the case of history, in particular, students bring with them memories of 'school history' – with its defining emphasis on dates and key political events. Now, the class encounters a new way of telling the past, one that includes more themes and groups – such as women and also working class histories – a 'crowding' or democratising of history: an approach that questions rather than prescribes (as in school), and encourages self-confidence as students consider the value of their personal or family stories. They learn that they have something to say.

Possibilities

The research does not end with the write-up. Students recount how their research has affected other family members – giving them a sense of their history and value. For others, the research is a starting point and they aim to add to it at a later stage or even to publish it. Ideally, publication would lead to an important source of biographical studies of help to the student, the researcher and the general reader. An initial attempt to publish student work is available in *Women's Studies Review.*[140] There is much possibility and there is also much interest.

The following section summarises briefly a sample of the research work of three students, written with permission from Maura, Mary and Yvonne.

Maura

Maura produced three pieces of research in women's history when studying for a Diploma in Women's Studies (County Clare). One study is of an emigrant woman to the United States in the mid-twentieth century, and is based on a collection of documents that Maura found in the attic of a house and in telephone interviews with the woman's daughters. It is a life history of a young woman learning to live in a new setting, in circumstances that enable a different telling of an emigration story.

The second study is of two women shopkeepers in a small County Clare town. This study is important in furthering our

---

[140] See, for example, Maria Luddy, "The Women's History Project." *Women's Studies Review,* Vol. 7. (Galway, 2000), 67-80.

knowledge about women in the commercial sector. An important category of women's work and, indeed, public position, it is barely considered in the research. For this study, Maura had a good range of public documents available to her, as well as interviews. On another thematic level, the findings also give valuable information about social roles, and status, of such women (not married) in a small town setting.

Maura's third piece of research – her final Diploma submission – was about her mother. In particular, she wanted to find out about her mother's role during the war of independence (1919-21). This story, based on military sources, interviews, local publications, census returns, school registers, and newspapers, is extremely well-researched. Neither – as Maura found on numerous occasions – was it straightforward; her mother's mobility as a child, for instance, made the tracking of her problematic; a local publication about the nationalist women's organisation, *Cumann na mBan*,[141] had no reference to her mother. Neither could she track down the reference to the prisoner that her mother had to visit as part of her work as a courier. It was a remarkable process of family memory coming into contact with documentary or official sources and, for Maura, trying to understand the disparity between the two. It was also an interesting exercise in trying to reconcile feminist thinking on *Cumann na mBan* (or, more generally, the phenomenon of women's auxiliary organisations), what Maura knew and had heard of her mother's activities, and what she was finding out through official sources.

Mary

A presentation that Mary submitted about a day in the life of her aunt is one of the student pieces published in the *Women's Studies Review* (Galway, 2000). It is an excellent summary of the various tasks and practices in the busy daily life of a rural mother. Its further importance, as in much of the work submitted by adult students, is that it documents a way of life that was common in rural working class Ireland until perhaps even the 1970s, but not now. Mary's Diploma year research about her urban (Dublin), working class family

---

[141] Women's Council formed in 1914 as an auxiliary to the nationalist male Volunteers. *Cumann na mBan* was organised more widely in response to the changing conditions in Ireland after 1916 (Rising), during the war of independence (1919-21) and the civil war (1922-1923).

contributes to another important, if little enough researched, area of Irish life. Living in the West made travel to Dublin not feasible, so we discussed using Dublin street directories (Thom's). She found this to be an inspiring method, enabling her to build up a picture of the various households on the street and to construct a clear image of the neighbourhood.

The resulting study is a testament to the hardship, courage and resourcefulness of working class Dublin in the mid-twentieth century. It is also a story of a woman – Mary's grandmother – who decides to end her life, an act of finality that was accentuated owing to her body not being recovered from the sea. What gives this project particular value is that it encouraged or helped Mary to try to resolve the story of her grandmother's death. The final chapter of this story, where Mary tracks down her grandmother's final resting place (in Scotland) and finds out that strangers there had commemorated this unknown woman, is itself a story of coincidence and certain symmetry.[142]

Yvonne

Yvonne, like Maura, contributed a number of pieces of research. In her first piece, she documented the life of her mother-in-law. This woman was an elected member of local government, a rare enough position in Ireland after the 1920s.[143] For her final Diploma project, Yvonne chose to investigate the life of her aunt Katy, who was an enormously important member of the family, having raised Yvonne's father.[144] She was, in effect, more grandmother than aunt. The starting point for the research was Katy the person or the woman. Yvonne was able to build up an initial picture of Katy's life by interviewing and consulting census material. Progress was discussed in class. The story took a different turn as Yvonne mentioned that Katy was also political, that she had been involved during the war of independence, but that she

---

[142] Mary is now pursuing a postgraduate degree. She told me of her additional findings after the course had ended and has given me permission to report on this story, which I much appreciate.

[143] The right to contest local government bodies was granted to Irishwomen during the 1890s and women were well-enough represented on the poor law boards and district councils up until c1925.

[144] In Ireland in the past – and this is another important theme – other family members raised a child if, for instance, a mother was ill after giving birth. Thus, women like Katy, who were single, were able to take up the role of the mother. (Single women could also foster workhouse children).

had never discussed the nature of her activities with her family. Interest and suggestions – from all in the group[145] – encouraged Yvonne to follow this up. The findings did, indeed, reveal that Katy was active – and reported on in the press – during the period in question; the story that Katy chose not to reveal. In a further complication to her aunt's life story, Yvonne found out that the state had refused to give a military pension to Katy.[146] And so another theme emerges as gender complicates how parliament (composed of former revolutionaries) calculates political effort in a post-independence period.

Final Comments

The value of doing research-based project work is exceptional, especially in the case of the learner returning to formal education; it is, in effect, the key to finding out what is important in the world of learning. To be able to decide a topic, to find information and to communicate those findings in a supportive environment leads to confidence and a sense of having a voice that is not so readily (or obviously) evident in conventional examination. The research project benefits the student, the tutor, the institution and the community. It also benefits the extended family when, for instance, various members supply memories, information, or artefacts in a collective attempt to make sense, understand and give credit to a member of the family.

Such work – as in so much of women's history-writing – leads the researcher into a personal, and sometimes, cathartic or emotional domain. There are practical results. As a result of her project research, one student now has an audio-tape of her mother that she would otherwise not have made, something that she values greatly. The same study drew in family members as they recalled information; it reached out to younger family members, listening and learning of people,

---

[145] This group was doing a piece of research to acquire the credits necessary to be granted a Diploma in Women's Studies, as they were not continuing to degree level. There were three students and myself as tutor. One of the students, Mary, died before the end of the course and was given a posthumous award. She was in her mid-eighties and an inspiring member of the class all along.

[146] In order to qualify for military pension, the applicant had to have a military identity. This was straightforward for men once they convinced the state that they had participated and came within the terms of the legislation. For the women who gave service to the cause of independence, the legislation was ambiguous and, sometimes, unrewarding.

practices and social issues that are mostly gone. Most importantly, in cases where the subject of the research is interviewed, the process gives to them an important intellectual space; they are now centre-stage, talking while others listen.

Bibliography

M. O'Dowd, M. MacCurtain and M. Luddy. "An Agenda for Women's History in Ireland, 1500-1900." *Irish Historical Studies.* **Vol. 28. No. 109. May, 1992.**
This detailed, analytical overview is an important synthesis of the various strands of scholarly enquiry that define the field of women's history in Ireland. The status of the compilers, who are pioneering scholars in the field, contribute to its value as a guide. Its broad scope is especially helpful in expanding the range of potential subject matter, questions and sources. The article remains a valuable resource in suggesting direction, and themes, to the contemporary researcher.

Siobhán Ní Bhrádaigh. *Mairéad Ní Ghráda: Ceannródaí Drámaíochta* **(1996). (Biography. Mairéad Ní Ghráda (1896-1971) – (in Irish).**
This biography offers an excellent insight into one of the early twentieth century pioneering, university educated women who were prominent in the social, intellectual, cultural and political life of Ireland. Ní Ghráda had a record of remarkable professional achievement, notably in radio broadcasting, writing school texts, editing educational journals and translating literature into Irish for children. Also a dramatist, one play, *An Triail* (1964) offers rare public status to the history of unmarried mothers during an era of stigma and punitive practice.

Saothar, the Journal of the Irish Labour History Society, publishes some articles and review essays relating to women's work, socialist women, oral histories of women workers and trade unionists. Its annual bibliography is excellent, with good reference to material on women. There is excellent opportunity for historians of women to use life stories and oral history to re-orient definitions of work and activism to include women. See, also, Caitríona Crowe. "Some Sources in the National Archives for Women's History." Vol. 19. (1994), 109-11; Monica Cullinan and Francis Devine. "Women and Labour History: A Select, Retrospective Bibliography, 1980-1995." Vol. 23. (1998), 133-141; and *Labour History News*, edited by Theresa Moriarty.

Maedhbh McNamara and Paschal Mooney. *Women in Parliament: Ireland: 1918-2000.* **Dublin: Wolfhound Press, 2000.**
Biographies, with photographs, of Irish women elected to parliaments in Westminster, Dublin, Belfast and Brussels. Introductory essays offer analysis of the roles and achievements of women in the context of Irish political behaviour and European trends. This biographical dictionary is a useful starting point for research into the lives of women in formal politics, though there is unevenness in the entries, and a tendency to define elected women in relation to fathers, brothers, sons and husbands. Indeed, it raises the challenge of how to explain and define the lives of political women, especially when belonging to a political family is a feature of political success.

Directory of Sources for the History of Women in Ireland. (CD-ROM and www.nationalarchives.ie/wh)
This Directory is the first major all-Ireland survey into sources for the history of women in Ireland. The Women's History Project, set up in 1997 with government support, contacted public and private repositories to find material for its database. The Directory contains an estimated 100,000 pieces of information about women in Ireland from earliest times to the present and is clearly an obvious research starting point. The project also publishes other material, such as collections of letters, photographs, a calendar of papers and surveys of government files. For details of its history, see, for instance, Maria Luddy. "The Women's History Project" in M. Clancy and C. Clear *et al.* eds. *Women's Studies Review.* Vol. 7. (Galway, 2000), 67-80. See, also, the extensive *Field Day Anthology of Irish Writing.* Vols. IV and V (Cork UP, 2002).

Textile Women Workers in Spain: IKE: A Case-study
María Suárez Lafuente

Illustration: Photos 'IKE workers ask for a way out' and 'the lonely workroom' in Carlos Prieto (ed.) IKE. Retales de la reconversión. (Madrid, Ladinamo Libros, 2004), 120, 143

Background

The rise and decline of the textile industry in Spain in the second half of the twentieth century constitutes a good field for the study of women's experience in the contemporary job market. With the opening of textile factories in the North of Spain in the 1950s, women found a means of surviving the decay of rural life and the meagre economy at home. It was the beginning of the *prêt-a-porter* (shirts, pants, raincoats) for the lower classes, and those factories flourished into the 1970s. After the oil crisis of 1974 and the subsequent changes in the economy map – led by a growth of multinational enterprises throughout the western world, a spectacular increase in the value of property, and the rise of political ventures in Spain as 'a plan with a future' – the old factories were no longer of interest for owners who saw their demise and subsequent replacement with apartment houses as the best economic option. The following example is a paradigm of such a 'development', but it not only illustrates the cold facts of economics, but highlights their effects on people, on the individual lives of the women who had worked in the factory, making it part of their biographies.

IKE

Confecciones Gijón was a shirt factory opened in 1952 in Gijón, an industrial city in the northern coast of Spain, situated in the Principality of Asturias. The workers of Confecciones Gijón were women, the supervisors and the owner were men. The firm brought out a type of shirt named IKE, in honour of the President of the United States, who had visited Spain and backed Franco – the shirt became so popular that the factory has been known as IKE ever since.

The factory owner came from the countryside and brought his workers mostly from his village; women who had no other future in a rural community than to find a husband to take care of them. These women provided excellent labour. They worked hard and were emotionally 'indebted' to the owner for giving them such an opportunity: they lived in the city, were able to rent a nice apartment with running water, and had money to buy clothes, go to the movies or sit in a café. Their gratefulness translated into high productivity, and, at its peak, the factory produced over a million shirts with no more than six hundred workers.

The relationship between the workers and the owner was archetypically patriarchal: workers regularly got an envelope with their salary and the master decided when to give them an extra incentive. There were presents at Christmas and on important occasions, and the master asked them personally about their health problems and about their family in the village. Once a year there was a day excursion and a meal paid for by 'the factory'.

Women felt that working in IKE was a privilege: they were taken care of and the factory was thriving. They embarked on mortgages to buy apartments and even cars, and when they went visiting in the village they were eyed with a mixture of envy and admiration. Their brothers, the inheritors of the land, mostly thought that their sisters had the better chance in life. Not being a loyal worker in Gijón was seen as an injury to the whole rural community in the village. This structure existed for more than twenty years.

In the early 1980s, the IKE shirts were no longer in fashion. Production fell, the master deviated money for other enterprises, and, for the first time in the history of the factory, workers were paid to leave their jobs, which some married women did. But this was only the beginning of the end. In 1986 the factory was declared impracticable in economic terms: the wise thing to do was to close it down, send the women home, tear down the building, sell the grounds for apartment houses, and get the reward for all those years of being such a good master. This had been the pattern in many other industrial concerns in Gijón over the previous eight to ten years: women went home with a monetary 'gratification' for their pains and fitted back into their archetypal slot, that of housewives – the adventure was over. But the women workers of Confecciones Gijón broke the pattern and wrote another page in women's history. They simply, and unexpectedly, said no to the master.

The Fight

At first, workers simply could not believe that this was happening to them, in their familial, predictable factory. They thought it not possible that their beloved master would allow something like that to happen to them, and felt the whole thing was a misunderstanding that would be promptly mended for them by whoever was going to be in charge. But time passed, things got worse and reality caught up with them – the workers either had to leave or stay and fight. Some more women left the factory and went home, but the rest, with no experience at all in syndicate dealings, organised themselves as best they could and started a resistance that lasted eight years, until 1994.

As a first measure they went on strike two days a week, to call some public attention to their problem – but neither society nor trade unions gave any credence to a bunch of women who, they considered, would do better by going back home and attending to their families; after all, if a woman loses her job nothing really happens, the problem is when a man loses his job, because then the family starves and the children are left without a future.

Very soon the IKE women were forced to start demonstrations, which blocked the streets, to remind the people of Gijón that they were still alive. They were not viewed with sympathy, and the police dispersed them with far more firmness than they did during other demonstrations of male workers from the coalmines or the shipyards. Nevertheless, and in spite of a couple of them being sent to hospital with lesser concussions, the IKE women escalated their protests: sit-ins in the middle of streets, tyre-burning across the highway, chaining themselves to the train to Madrid to retard its departure, taking over public buildings in the middle of the morning - all to no real effect. Some official measures were taken, but more to appease the workers and send them home than to help the factory to be productive again. But the workers were not to be fooled. After a fruitless round of talks with different politicians, they retained by force, during several hours in the factory premises, two directors from the board, and went to Madrid to occupy the Cuban Embassy in the (vain) hope that they would be more sympathetic towards workers.

In June 1990, all hope of any help from official sources were lost, and some three hundred women decided to live in the factory, round the clock, to avoid it being emptied of machines and material, which they saw as the only hope left of ever being able to resume textile production. They thought the police would send them out within twenty four hours, but, to their surprise, they were left in peace and the sit-in lasted four years.

Life in the factory was hard, but unique. The women learnt to organise in an intimate community; they learnt to share, they learnt about sorority, about feminism, about themselves, about their families. They experienced all kind of feelings. Some were backed by their families, some were despised, some were forced to serve three shifts (family, factory and street resistance). Time stretched for better and for worse: Christmases, birthdays and anniversaries succeeded one another and were celebrated by workers and families within the factory premises. Backs survived sleeping on mattresses on the floor, and the fear of being alone at night, expecting to be expelled by force at any time, was also conquered with the passing of time.

In 1991, the IKE women decided to form a political all-women-list to run for the coming elections for Mayor of Gijón (300,000 inhabitants) and for the Presidency of Asturias (one million inhabitants). They only aspired to be noticed, to signal to a dormant society that they were still alive and fighting. *IKE-Women Against the Dole* made politicians feel very uneasy, the Socialist Party in power promised to make the factory viable once more, and the Communist Party saw its usually small number of votes be dangerously challenged. The purpose of the list was fulfilled amply, even though the socialist promise never eventuated.

In 1994, after scaring away possible buyers in three previous auctions, the workers themselves succeeded in acquiring the factory at a public auction. But the factory and the firm were ruined after such a long time, so the workers sold the property for development purposes and divided the money among those who resisted until the end, and also those who left between 1986 and 1994. Nevertheless, since they had not been able to keep the factory and the jobs going, the IKE women experienced a sense of failure, even though they had, indeed, achieved an enormous personal and social victory.

Summary

The fight of the IKE women against masters and politicians was important for several reasons. Most women were only twelve years old when they started working (fourteen years old was the official working age at that time). This means that they were not educated, and many of them first menstruated sitting on the working stool. It was easy, therefore, to turn them into 'good, passive workers' and to create a strong bond between them and the 'factory ideology'. So, the subsequent problems, the defection of the owner and their own disenchantment with the system, constituted a social awakening for those meek, hard-working women.

Accustomed to being within the shelter of the factory eight hours a day and spending time with fellow workers or family, the IKE women had to face not only a revolt against their masters, but also the challenge of going out into the streets – into the public domain – and making themselves notorious: shouting, constructing barricades and standing up to the police forces. Several women now confess nauseas and panic attacks the night before going out on demonstrations. Such activities, as well as the sit-in in the factory over a four year period, where activities involved mainly sitting around, reading and talking to the other women workers, provoked a personal reflection about the aims in their lives and their plans for a future that had to be different. Most women were then in their forties and had children still at school.

Analysing the changes in their lives over the previous six to eight years, as well as the drastic changes to their sense of security and permanence, the IKE women experienced the pros and cons of personal and communal empowerment. A sense of empowerment that had been so hard won that it was an achievement in itself: they might not have won the fight in the end, but at least they were not easy to defeat. They certainly were not 'the weak and fair sex', and the bonding with the other workers helped them to experience 'sorority'. With time to reflect, they surprised themselves: they were shocked to realise that they were feared by the police, by politicians and by other factory owners, and also to know that they had become a popular icon in Asturias. Self-esteem grew considerably in many cases.

Teaching Aids
Press releases;
Photographs;
Aritha Van Herk's ficto-graphic article on the IKE problem;
Interviews with the women.

8.   **'Digital Foremothers in a City in Female Hands': A Didactic Project in Malines (Belgium)**

Laurence Claeys, Sonja Spee

Illustration: Webpage from http://www.mechelen2005.be "Digital foremothers in a city in female hands"

Introduction

Gendering space and constructing gendered forms of commemoration practices were among the aims of early feminist projects. Marking the space with monuments, giving the name of women to streets and squares are crucial to think about how men and women differently contributed to past achievements and how these achievements are valued and remembered by later generations. Analysing these practices and instances we get to know how gendered memory works, connecting personal and institutional forms of memory.

Description of the Project

In 2005 Malines was called "a city in female hands" (http://www.mechelen2005.be). During this 'female year', the town was enlivened by exhibitions, performing arts, festive activities and conferences about women or by women, where womanhood was stereotyped and empowering, but ubiquitous. On the sidelines, more social-artistic and social-cultural activities developed, like the 'Digital Foremothers' project, developed by the Policy Research Centre on Equal Opportunities. The idea of a 'Digital Foremothers' project was inspired by the experiences of the Digital Foremothers project of Berteke Waaldijk and Andrea Pető during the NOISE Summer School in Antwerp (2003), as well as by other digital oral history projects (http://www.bna-bbot.be/db2/).

The Construction of the Female Face of the City

The proposition to work around his/her/story and foremothers in secondary schools with a strong emphasis on digitalisation was embraced by the Urselinen, a secondary school in Malines. Different partners were involved in the development of a 'Digital mothers' database, website and event (www.digitalevoormoeders.be).

Participation from the Urselinen consisted of 3 teachers (history, informatics and fashion) and 47 students from the fifth grade (15-16 year). The students learned interview methods, were informed on the historical context of the living conditions of their foremothers and on oral history, and up-graded their digital skills. With this knowledge the students interviewed their foremothers (grandmothers, female neighbours, nuns, female role models). They gathered pictures of the life of their foremother, made transcripts of the interviews and, finally, constructed their 'digital foremother'.

One teacher, from the Higher Education for Information-management and Information-system, accepted the challenge to develop, with his students, a database, search engine and interface for the website of the 'Digital Foremothers'. These students gave a workshop at the Urselinen to teach the secondary school students skills relating to the digitalisation of their interviews, scanning of pictures, learning HTML, and uploading to server, etc. The Centre for Cultural Inheritance, known for its work on local oral history, helped the teachers by developing the interview script in a way that meant it could be used for different purposes. They also edited the interviews and published some of them in a local magazine.

Results

The enthusiasm of all of the partners made the project the success that it was. Only a small financial budget was available for the final event. During this event, the 'Digital Foremothers' website was presented to the public of Malines so that everyone could experience the stories of the foremothers. Students of the Urselinen held a fashion parade during which they dressed as their foremothers would have, a foremother was surfing on the just-developed website, and Sonja Spee gave a theoretical lecture on oral his/herstory. In the future, the different Centres for Cultural Inheritance of the Flemish Community of Belgium are planning on using this format in different cities because of the added values of the intergenerational aspect, the conservation of local (female) inheritance, the use of new media, and the positive pedagogical implications of the project.

9.   *'Angels in the Nurseries': A Poem that Sheds Light on the History of Women*
Marie-Louise Carels

Illustration: Heading of a Prospectus
for Founding a Day Nursery in Liège (Belgium) 1847
(Property of the Municipality of Liège,
Echevinat des Services Sociaux et de la famille)

Introduction

Why would we use a poem written by a man (Marcel Briol) to introduce a history of women? Because it presents two nineteenth century women workers who offer praise for a day-care centre for their babies, which makes it possible for them to go to work and, thus, ward off poverty, and because the poem also celebrates the wealthy patronesses who provided resources for the nurseries. The issue of caring for children is closely related to women's working lives – whether as mothers who have to leave their babies or as child-minders whose work it is to look after other women's children.

Context

The poem was found during our research into the historical conditions of child-minding among the lower classes in the Liège region (Belgium). A specific question had initiated our research: why do women have a negative image of day nurseries even if they have never used or visited one? It was obvious to us,[147] as psycho-educationalists involved in research work with women's associations aiming to raise the general awareness about the need for child-care facilities, that part of the answer was probably to be found in the history of such facilities, associated as they were with aid extended to the needy. A work group consisting of historians, sociologists, psychologists, social workers and child minders (all women)[148] set out to reconstruct the history of day-care centres and of the women who used them.

In 1980 the project was innovative, since the history of women was not yet a fashionable subject and interest in oral history was only at an early stage. We had to start from scratch since no research on this topic existed in Belgium. We also had to study the context, namely the working conditions for women of the lower classes in the Liège region, and establish what protection there was for mothers and children.

Our project was, of course, based on archives,[149] but also on iconographic documents such as photographs and postcards. In order to make room for a private form of history and listen to people who are generally left out of the official and formal history, we also interviewed elderly women: former women workers (born between 1900 and 1910) who worked at Fabrique Nationale d'armes at Herstal, a weapon-making company that employed a majority of women in a borough where there was no day-care facility.[150] We also interviewed

---

[147] The author and her colleague, Gentile Manni, research coordinators, U of Liège (Belgium).

[148] The names of the team members are as follows: Anne-Marie Alestra, Suzanne Bohet, Dominique Cuppens, Sonia Debauque, Michèle Huberty, Ginette Letawe, Astrid Manni, Chantal Marée, Anna Secchi.

[149] Suzanne Bohet, *Les crèches en région liégeoise*, (Day Nurseries in the Liège Region) (U of Liège, 1980), unpublished document; Dominique Lafontaine, *Maternité et Petite enfance dans le bassin industriel liégeois de 1830 à 1940*, (Maternity and Infancy in the Liège industrial area 1830-1940) (U of Liège, 1984), unpublished document.

[150] Astrid Manni *et al.*, *En ce temps là Elisabeth... Des femmes de la F.N. témoignent*, (In those days Elisabeth... Women Workers at the FN testify) (U of Liège, 1980), unpublished document.

mothers who entrusted their children to a town day-care centre, at Laveu (Liège) between 1920 and 1940.[151]

For the purposes of this exercise, instead of the selected poem, we could have used those interviews, in which women actually talk less about the nurseries (into which they could not go for sanitary reasons) than about their everyday lives as women, mothers, workers and about what their parents' lives had been like. Instead, we chose to focus on one of the documents found by the historians in our team, namely Marcel Briol's poem called "Les anges des crèches" ("Angels in the Nurseries"). Indeed, on the basis of this somewhat unexpected source, we can address both sense and sensibility to raise our awareness of the history of women.

The Source

The source was located in a book by Marcel Briol, *Aux dames de Liège. Les cœurs d'or ou le triomphe de la charité*,[152] the second book of which is devoted to the "Angels in the Nurseries". The poem, which covers twelve pages and is written in the style of the time, consists of five parts:[153]

- o Envoi aux dames patronnesses de l'œuvre des crèches (Envoy to the Patronesses Donating to Nurseries)
- o Prologue. Le bataillon sacré (Prologue. The Heavenly Batallion)
- o 1°partie Bethléem (Part 1: Bethlehem)
- o 2°partie Liège (Part 2: Liège)
- o Epilogue. La phalange terrestre (Epilogue. The Earthly Battalion)

In the part entitled "Liège", the writer presents two women workers talking to each other early in the morning:

"Anne, vous le savez, mon âme est à l'épreuve,

[151] Marie-Louise Carels, *A la crèche en 1930, des mères témoignent*, (In a Nursery in 1930, mothers testify) (U of Liège, 2005), unpublished document.

[152] Marcel Briol, "Aux dames de Liège. Les cœurs d'or ou le triomphe de la charité," in *Souvenir poétique du Carnaval de 1864*, (To the Ladies of Liège. Hearts of Gold or Charity Triumphant), (Liège, 1864).

[153] The whole poem can be read in Suzanne Bohet, 1980.

A peine en mes vingt ans, Dieu m'a fait mère et veuve;
Je pleure chaque jour mais ne le maudis pas
Sans cet enfant chéri j'eus connu le trépas
(...)
Je ne vous dirai pas tout ce que j'ai souffert
Mais un beau jour j'appris qu'une oeuvre charitable
Ouvrait pour le malheur un abri secourable.
L'asile que fondait la sainte CHARITE,
N'avait rien de blessant ! - point de mendicité !
Point de honte, non pas ! - ce n'est pas une aumône,
C'est l'hospitalité qu'à bon droit on vous donne.
(...)
(You know, Anne, my dear, how hard life is on me:
I am barely twenty, and mother and widow;
Though I weep every day our God I never curse
Without my beloved child I would be in my grave.
(...)
Impossible to tell all I've had to go through
But then some day I heard that some charity work
Provided for the poor a much needed shelter.
The help we can receive from such blessed CHARITY
Cannot hurt our pride,- it's not mendacity!
No shame attached to it!- no alms are handed down
But hospitality we are entitled to.)

In the Epilogue he celebrates the women who support this enterprise:

"Oui vous prêtez à Dieu! naïves jeunes filles,
En consacrant ici vos talents au malheur;
Car vous venez en aide aux mères de familles
En donnant à l'enfance un abri protecteur".
(To God indeed you lend! ye innocent maidens,
As you devote your skills to alleviate pain;
For you help out mothers who else were tied and fast
When you provide shelters for their babies in arms.)

Thus, the text is a call both to women workers who had to entrust their children to nurseries and also to the well-off women who supported those facilities.

We have only found two such poems in the Liège region, but it seems that they were fairly common in philanthropic societies, as is suggested by Catherine Bouve in her study of French day nurseries.[154] These songs and poems were addressed to the elite and did not question the Establishment; they merely aimed at prompting more patrons to donate freely. As underlined by Bouve, the theme of angels is pervasive in poems on nurseries, (cribs), with a play on the word 'angel' referring both to the infant guests and to the lady donors.

How We Propose to Use the Poem
However *passé*, this kind of text, which attempted to make the well-off aware of the distress experienced by the poor, can still move students and teachers who feel concerned by either history or education; on this basis they could be encouraged to raise questions about the history of women. Indeed, starting from this poem, or others of the same kind, we can trace several lines of enquiry. The history of the nurseries, which were social-minded though patronising endeavours, but also a world of women.

In France, those day-care facilities where babies were looked after were created by Firmin Marbeau (1798-1875) in 1844 and called 'crèches'[155] after the crib in which the newborn Jesus was laid.[156] As a charitable organisation that offers help and shelter to the poor they

---

[154] Catherine Bouve, "*La poésie comme contribution à une compréhension socio-historique du projet des crèches collectives.*" (Poetry as Contribution to a Socio-historical Understanding of the Setting Up of Collective Day Care Centres), in *Forum, Revue de la recherche en sciences sociales*, 105, (2004), 31-39; Catherine Bouve's analysis focuses on the work of Etienne Deschamps (1791-1871), a Romantic French poet, vice-president of the *Société des crèches* (France).

[155] In French, the word 'crèche' is used for the place where the mothers entrust their children (nurseries) and for the place where Jesus was born.

[156] "a pure and holy place," said Firmin Marbeau in *Des crèches, ou moyen de diminuer la misère en augmentant la population*. (On Nurseries, or How to Fight Poverty and Raise Population Figures), (Paris, Comptoir des imprimeurs-Unis, 1845). It is the first book ever written on nurseries. It has been reprinted six times and translated into various languages. In the Epilogue, Marcel Briol thanks the municipality of Liège as follows:
"*Imitant Bethléem dans ses jours d'allégresse*
Liège chante aujourd'hui la Crèche avec ivresse(...)
(Vying with Bethlehem in days of rejoicing
Liège is celebrating its Crèche and carolling)

belonged to a form of social utopia, the aim of which was to reconcile social classes. They were founded by men,[157] patrons and philanthropists, but the actual work was carried out by women, whether patronesses who collected money and saw to the proper management of the facilities, or *berceuses* (rocking women), which is what the women who looked after the children were first called, before they became *soigneuses* (minders), *éleveuses* (upbringers), and finally *puéricultrices* (nursery nurses).

The day-care centres were intended for lower-class children, but they also functioned as 'schools for mothers' since they taught working class women the rudiments of cleanliness, orderliness and good behaviour, thus contributing to the 'moralising' of the lower classes, and women in particular. "Day nurseries tell the poor mother (…). Now you can work, but mind you behave, for I will not harbour vice. (…) They tell the charitable funds (…) We fight poverty in its three main sources: bad health, immorality, and lack of cleanliness."[158]

From the very beginning, nurseries were a source of controversy: in Liège,[159] as in France,[160] archives (municipal reports, newspaper articles, etc.) contain heated discussions around health issues: do nurseries rescue children from poverty, perhaps even death, or do they favour epidemics? Physicians argued as much on this topic as on the desirability of breast-feeding. Conflicts also arose as to who nurseries were for: are they only intended for working women or for families in difficult social circumstances? Morality interfered: should the children of unmarried mothers be taken in? Positions on such issues vary according to the political views of municipal representatives (all of them men), and this is reflected in opinions about whether access to the facilities should be free or not.

---

[157] "Noble charity, this virile virtue," Briol wrote.

[158] Firmin Marbeau, *Des crèches pour les petits enfants des ouvrières*, (Nurseries for the babies of working women), (Paris, 1863), 5th edition.

[159] Suzanne Bohet (1984).

[160] Catherine Bouve, *Les crèches collectives : usagers et représentations sociales. Contribution à une sociologie de la petite enfance,* (Collective Day Care Centres: Users and Social Image. Contribution to a Sociology of Early Childhood), (Paris: L'Harmattan, coll. Le travail du social, 2004).

Fields of Enquiry

- o the history of charity and its (male and female) agents;
- o living and working conditions among working class people, particularly women, in the nineteenth century and at the beginning of the twentieth century;
- o changes in the occupations of mothers who leave their children in a nursery;
- o changes in the occupations perceived as suited to women since the nineteenth century;
- o the impact of religion in the founding and daily management of those facilities. Catherine Bouve points, for instance, to some similarity between the function of the *berceuses* and probationers at a convent.
- o Religion also influenced women's everyday lives. In Belgium in the 1930s, several legal measures promoted by the Christian trade union and political party aimed at restricting or even prohibiting work for married women;
- o the part played by physicians in conveying middle class morality among the working class, the role of nurses and midwives;[161]
- o contraception and abortion practices, which were prohibited and, consequently, kept secret;
- o day-care centres as a hot issue related to the status of women and to women at work;[162]
- o the diversity and development of arguments for and against corporate nurseries (the issue is still debated today);
- o the apparent contradiction between the image of the ideal nineteenth century woman as wife and mother and the founding of nurseries to help working women;[163]

---

[161] See Luc Boltanski, *Prime Education et morale de classe.* (Prime Education and Class Morality), (Dijon : de l'Ecole des Hautes études en sciences sociales, 1969).

[162] Marie-Louise Carels and Gentile Manni, "*De l'enfant désiré à la crèche de nos désirs,*" (From the Desired Child to the Nursery We Desire) in Cahiers du GRIF, *Les femmes et les enfants d'abord,* (Bruxelles, décembre 1975), 9-10.

[163] Eliane Gubin et Valérie Piette, "*Mères au travail, mères au foyer: les controverses de l'entre-deux-guerres,*" (Working Mothers, Mothers at Home: controversy between the wars') in Godelieve Masuy-Strobant and Perrine Humblet, *Mères et nourrissons. De la bienfaisance à la protection médico-sociale (1830—1945).* (Mothers and Babies. From Charity to Social and Medical Security 1830-1945), (Bruxelles : Labor, 2004).

- o the current debate opposing direct financial assistance to families and the funding of facilities for working women.
- o The field of day child-minding centres for international comparisons. For instance, we can wonder why the use of 'wet nurses' seems to have been much more wide-spread in France than in Belgium,[164] and why nurseries in Britain were still only available to working class mothers in the 1990s.[165]
- o Surveying the history of child-minding, analysing the development in child nursing standards and in education guidelines, which placed mothers (and nurses) in a practical double-bind should be an interesting object of study, especially for future nurses.[166]
- o Surveys asking parents how they perceive day-care nurseries today have been carried out with students in psychology and pedagogical sciences. The ground has been prepared by students remembering their own infant days (at home or in a nursery, with grandparents or with a minder?), and wondering about reasons for respective choices. Surveys among parents bring out how roles are still distributed between fathers and mothers.[167]

Another project of ours is to launch a historical survey among people working in nurseries that would revolve around the key date of 1970 when, in Belgium at least, nurseries were no longer perceived as 'charity institutions' for working class people, but as a service for all families. Marcel Briol's poem will be used as a starting point for students' enquiries and debates. (Translations by Christine Pagnoulle, Doctor of English literacy, Member of FER-ULg)

---

[164] Vincent Gourdon and Catherine Rollet, "*Modèles français, modèles belges, un jeu de miroirs,*" ('French Models, Belgian Models-mirroring effects') in Godelieve Masuy-Strobant and Perrine Homblet, *op. cit.*

[165] Marie-Louise Carels and Gentile Manni, "*Quels éducateurs pour des lieux d'accueil de qualité. Un éclairage européen,*" ("What kind of tutors for quality minding. A European approach"). *Education* (Special issue), 1990, 217/218, 60-7.

[166] See, for example, Geneviève Delaisi de Parseval and Suzanne Lallemand, *L'art d'accommoder les bébés. 100 ans de recettes françaises de puériculture,* (How to Accommodate Babies. 100 years of French Recipes in Child Minding), (Paris: Seuil, 1980).

[167] See, also, Catherine Bouve's analysis: as they entrust their babies to a nursery, mothers relinquish to other women the educational tasks which are traditionally regarded as their own.

10. *Teaching a Social Work Module Using Students' Memories*
Vivienne Bozalek

Illustration: Students doing Participatory Action Research methods at Social Work Department, University of the Western Cape, South Africa

Introduction

This teaching and research project was prompted by my own dissatisfaction with traditional texts in the field of Child and Family Care in social work used by South African higher education institutions. Students at the University of the Western Cape (UWC), a historically disadvantaged institution in Cape Town where I have been working for the past fifteen years, also expressed to me in interviews how inappropriate they found these texts for their practical work, based as they were on old-fashioned functionalist ideas. I then set out to find a way to include family histories, through the memories of family life of the students in the social work classes on Child and Family Care that I was teaching. The results of this project have been published as my dissertation (Utrecht University, 2004). The following article describes the project and concludes with some

199

recommendations for social work curricula. It is based on a summary of the dissertation.

Description

A look at the traditional texts used in teaching social work Child and Family Care reveals the implicit assumptions and value judgements underlying such texts, such as the normality of the nuclear family, prescribed roles that family members should take, and what the role of social worker should be. The ideas expressed in traditional texts on 'the family', which present as neutral, scientific accounts of a family situation, are presented to students as authoritative accounts and texts and are very influential in determining what is do-able and thinkable in relation to social work with families. In order to develop a more relevant social work curriculum in South Africa, I wanted to discover what insights the UWC students' own written accounts on their family circumstances from the perspective of race, gender and generation, could have for the social work curriculum.

When I started teaching the course on Child and Family Care, I decided to collect the written assignments that UWC students conducted on their own families and to examine their relevance for the curriculum. To this end, I had, together with a group of third year social work students at UWC, worked on and changed an assignment in relation to the students' families of origin, which was already being used as part of the fieldwork curriculum. The changes made included the incorporation of life histories on family members, as well as questions on how different forms of racism–cultural, institutional and personal–affected students and their family members, the gendered division of labour and how various categories of people, such as women, men, children and the elderly, were positioned in family practices. Students were given a course reader, which encouraged a more critical view of family issues, the influence of social policy and reflected South African realities. Students conducted research on their families during the long summer holidays – they were the primary researchers in collecting the data. Over a period of approximately six years, I collected 118 assignments from students who gave me permission to use their work for the purposes of research and teaching. The title of my dissertation – recognition, resources, responsibilities – refers to the three approaches that are pertinent to the social work curriculum in that they encompass a social justice and ethics of care perspective. These three approaches reflect Nancy Fraser's notion of recognition, the human capabilities approach developed by Amartya Sen and Martha Nussbaum, and the feminist political ethics of care approach developed by Joan Tronto and Selma Sevenhuijsen.

The questions that I posed were:
> what could students and their family members do and be in relation to the social markers of race, gender and generation.
> How were they advantaged or disadvantaged in terms of these markers and what implications did this have for them in their lives?
> Were they able to interact on a par or an equal basis with others in their lives?
> How did they fare in relation to being able to give and receive care in situations of their own choice?

My theoretical framework enabled me to come to conclusions about how well students and their family members were flourishing in light of these questions. The major findings of this study show the ways in which students understood cultural and institutional racism in relation to their own situations and the sorts of family practices that developed in relation to these forms of racism, as well as the way gender and generation affected family practices.

The concept of cultural racism, which I view as an instance of misrecognition, a concept developed by Nancy Fraser, proved very useful. Students and their family members have reported that their cultural practices and values have been devalued or demeaned in various ways. The students' accounts speak about these experiences in terms of 'primitivisation', 'othering' and 'inferiorisation'. Students reported that they and their family members were 'primitivised' or regarded as less developed and being lower on the evolutionary ladder in a number of different contexts – the impact of Christianity on their religious practices, how 'primitivisation' effected family members in their paid work situation, and how ethnic markers influenced 'primitivity' – with those marked as African being regarded primitive, dangerous and cruel by those marked as coloured.

Students' accounts also showed how they were 'othered' as a form of cultural racism. By 'othered', I mean how they were regarded as 'them' or 'objects' rather than 'us' or 'subjects' – how they were regarded as unimportant. I also made use of the human capabilities approach to present the students' accounts of how this form of racism affected themselves and their family members. 'Inferiorisation' refers to how family members were regarded as mentally, physically or emotionally inferior to the accepted norm. I used Val Plumwood's notion of dualism to examine the means by which students, in their accounts, identify how they are misrecognised. One of these mechanisms – 'backgrounding' – which is the denial of dependency on subordinated others, is a theme that came through strongly in students' accounts, where time and again there were instances of their family members having been used in various ways to fulfil the needs of those who occupied more privileged positions, but with no acknowledgement or recognition of this situation.

Students' accounts show how the various contexts of education, paid employment, and religious practices can be regarded as instances of 'inferiorisation' and 'othering', and the effects that this had on family members and their practices, as well as how differently situated people, for example, the older and younger generations, reacted to 'inferiorisation'. Familism was also regarded by students to be a form of cultural racism, in the white insistence on the nuclear family as the desired norm.

Students' accounts also reveal how, on the basis of racial markers, more than any other form of categorisation, people were deliberately excluded from access to resources, in ways largely outside their control, resulting in compounded effects on family practices. Students' reports showed how institutional racism went far beyond simply depriving students and their family members from resources, but brutally dispossessed them of their resources and destroyed relationships. Having their resources confiscated had many implications for students and their families. These implications, which are exemplified time after time in their accounts, include physical separation of kin and neighbours from each other, as well as wrenching people from their homes and communities, with which they strongly identified, and removing their animals and livestock. In this way, linkages between people, as well as who and what they found valuable, were disrupted and destroyed. The policies that prevented African students' family members from moving freely from rural to urban areas, and criminalised family members through arrests for Pass Laws, were also deeply damaging in terms of people's physical, mental and material well-being. These policies made the bodies of students' family members into public property, which undermined their sense of personal integrity.

Students' reports show how, in terms of the lack of these capabilities, this affected their family practices and their lives fell far short of conditions beneficial for human development. It was not just that this was reported to have occurred, but in a multitude of forms of racialised exclusion, which, together, destroyed social structures and support systems through a range of public policies and practices. Lack of access to education led to poverty, which, in turn, led to an inability to gain access to education, which was compounded by an inferior education system available to black students, which further impacted upon family members' impoverishment. The lack of, and inadequate, housing available to black families, as well as the conditions under which they lived, were further debilitating factors, as were racialised restrictions on employment opportunities and the denial of access to recreational facilities. However, it is the system of forced removals that seems, in students' accounts, to have been regarded as the most pernicious, having had the effect of destroying people's homes, taking away their property, assets and land, destroying bonds between people, preventing them from practising important religious rituals, and displacing people from loved and familiar places to strange ones without infrastructure and access to employment. Students' responses to how they and their family members coped with institutional racism fell into six broad categories: the first was through family members supporting each other in the face of institutional racism; the second was resignation, which took two forms – either an avoidance of situations in which they were discriminated against, or acceptance of the situation through different kinds of rationalisation, for example, belief in God's salvation for their suffering; thirdly, students described collective forms of coping with institutional racism where they joined fellow workers, members of their communities, or political organisations to challenge and attempt to change their circumstances; fourth were forms of self-destructive behaviour, such as alcohol and drug use and abuse, and violence towards family members; fifth was hatred of whites as perpetrators of institutional racism, as well as those regarded as privileged on account of it existence; sixth was a response of reconciliation and forgiveness towards those who had denied students and their family members access to resources.

The students' accounts, which can be seen as appropriations of contested spaces in social work, are important for the curriculum in two ways: firstly, in the identification and acknowledgement of the impact of institutional racism and its multiple effects on their lives and those of their family members, which, in itself, is significant in contesting invisibility and denial of these effects, and, secondly, in the recognition of their methods of coping with and being able to survive institutional racism.

Conclusions

Gender and generation were shown to have an important impact upon students and their family members. Students reported on the responsibilities that family members undertook to ensure their survival, as well as how categories of people were positioned and the effects this had on their ability to flourish, and how resources were distributed amongst categories of people in the household. As an analytical tool, I used the feminist political ethic of care, which sees the work involved in care as central to the human experience and re-valorises care as a social practice. The approach problematises the neo-liberal notion of the self-sufficient individual who does not need or make use of care. And it acknowledges that, as persons, we are all dependent and vulnerable – we all need and use care and are all potentially capable of giving care. Responsibilities highlighted in students' accounts included household tasks such as cooking, cleaning, outside work, care-giving activities, as well as economic activities to ensure the survival of family members. These responsibilities would all be considered forms of care in that they take as a starting point for action another person's needs and incorporate the actual hands-on work of care-giving and taking care of. In terms of social categories, it was largely women and girl children (mothers, grandmothers, aunts and siblings) who did the hands-on care-giving work, while all members of the family, especially both parents, but also siblings, contributed their efforts to bringing in resources to family members through paid employment.

From the accounts it also emerged that the needs of care-givers were largely ignored by those whose needs were being met. Because these family members spent a great deal of their time meeting other family members' needs, they were not able to participate on an equal footing, as their own needs were not being met by someone else, and they did not have the time to pursue other activities. For example, girl children were reported to have been unable to accomplish homework tasks because of the responsibilities they undertook relating to cooking, cleaning and looking after younger siblings. Where the data revealed exceptions to these situations, they were analysed in terms of the notion of 'gender traitors'. These unusual circumstances, where men engaged in care-giving, are examples that can be flagged for students and used to show how the presumed naturalness of categories of gender and generation can be resisted or rejected and their assumed privileges interrogated.

Gender and generation have been shown to be very influential in how students and family members are appreciated or unappreciated, in how they are valued or devalued. Seniority, according to students' accounts, brought with it respect and authority. Women's differential subject positions as daughters-in-law, mothers, and paid workers also had significance in terms of recognition or misrecognition. Men's and children's positions, as family members, were influenced by how they were regarded, and by family practices which emanated from these perceptions.

What emerged from students' accounts is that participatory parity, in other words, acting as equals or peers with kin, was rarely achieved for culturally devalued categories such as children and women. There was neither equal respect for the attributes ascribed to these categories, nor were there opportunities for them to develop themselves so that they could achieve social esteem.[168] From students' accounts, what they and their family members could aspire to depended on social categories such as gender and generation. For example, what women and children as family members could desire, say or do was different from what men and elders could desire, say or

---

[168] Fraser (1997).

do. What students made clear in their accounts was that it was culturally unthinkable for women or children to desire certain things, for example, to have their needs prioritised above those who are more valued, and that, therefore, they would not contemplate this as a possibility.

What also became clear is that cognisance must be taken by social workers that one cannot assume that as members of devalued categories or subject positions, women and children will be willing or able to simply express their views of what they may want or 'claim the rights' to which they are entitled. The differential or unequal access to household resources, such as food, affected family members' lives, in terms of ethnicity, gender and generation. In terms of which family members flourished and who struggled to survive, gender and generation were shown to be quite influential. Younger members of the family were more vulnerable in that they were not accorded much voice or resources and had to do what was expected of them by adults. A situation of gerontocracy prevailed, with elders being revered in almost all situations. Female family members also largely found themselves in positions of accessing fewer or less adequate resources and having more responsibilities than male family members.

The aim of this research has been to formulate recommendations from these findings for renewing the social work curriculum in South Africa. My conclusion is that students' accounts offer important insights for the curriculum into the identification and acknowledgement of the impact of wider social forces, such as racism, gender and generation, on the micro-practices of people's lives. The introduction of students' accounts of their gendered and racialised experiences have allowed me to make changes to the social work curriculum. The following recommendations for the renewal of the social work curriculum emanated from this study: it is important to interrogate the assumptions underlying texts and concepts used in social work courses, the concept of misrecognition and the mechanisms by which misrecognition is achieved is of crucial importance in curriculum content dealing with assessment, intervention and evaluation by social work educators.

Finally, the students' accounts will allow teachers to replace an emphasis on abuse with an emphasis on care-giving, and allow them to incorporate a concept of exclusion from a human capabilities perspective in the teaching. Participatory research techniques or Participatory Action Learning in the curriculum of social work education is, therefore, of the greatest importance to operationalise learning from this research project on students' memories of their families.

Contributors

- ❖ Vivienne Bozalek, Associate Professor, Chairperson, Social Work Department, University of the Western Cape, South Africa.
- ❖ Marie-Louise Carels, Researcher at the Training and Education Department of the University of Liège, Member of Femmes-Enseignement-Recherche Université de Liège, Belgium.
- ❖ Patricia Chiantera Stutte, Assistant Professor, University of Bari, Italy.
- ❖ Laurence Claeys, PhD student, University of Antwerp, Belgium.
- ❖ Mary Clancy, Lecturer, Women's Studies Centre, National University of Ireland, Galway.
- ❖ Erla Hulda Halldorsdottir, PhD student, Centre for Research in the Humanities, Researcher at the Centre for Gender Studies, University of Iceland.
- ❖ Martine Jaminon, Maison de la Science of Liège and University of Liège, Belgium.
- ❖ Redi Koobak, Assistant Lecturer, Department of English, University of Tartu, Estonia.
- ❖ Leena Kurvet-Käosaar, Researcher, Department of Literature and Folklore, University of Tartu, Estonia.
- ❖ Ritva Nätkin, Acting Professor, University of Tampere, Finland.
- ❖ Andrea Pető, Associate Professor, Department of Gender Studies, Central European University, Budapest, University of Miskolc, Hungary.
- ❖ Giovanna Providenti, Researcher, Università Roma Tre, Rome, Italy.
- ❖ Sonja Spee, Senior Researcher, University of Antwerp, Belgium.
- ❖ Lada Stevanovic, PhD student, ISH, Ljubljana, Slovenia.
- ❖ María Suárez Lafuente, Professor, University of Oviedo, Spain.
- ❖ Berteke Waaldijk, Professor, University of Utrecht, The Netherlands.